THE WORD THROUGH SOUND

THE WORD THROUGH SOUND

Making Sense of Matthew's Gospel
Through Music

STEVE ADAMS

Authentic

First published 2004 by Authentic Media, 9 Holdom Avenue, Bletchley, Milton Keynes,
Bucks, MK1 1QR, UK and PO Box 1047, Waynesboro, GA 30830-2047, USA.

08 07 06 05 04   7 6 5 4 3 2 1

British Library Cataloguing in Publication Data
A catalogue record for this book is available from the British Library.

1-86024-472-6

Cover design by David Lund
Printed in Great Britain by CPD (Wales), Ebbw Vale

CONTENTS

CD TRACK LISTING

Session 1: 'Paralyzed'
taken from the album *Divine Discontent* by Sixpence None the Richer
(Word Entertainment, 2002)

Session 2: 'Still Burning'
taken from the album *Divine Discontent* by Sixpence None the Richer
(Word Entertainment, 2002)

Session 3: 'You Don't Have To'
taken from the album *Take Back the Beat* by The Tribe
(Alliance Music, 2001)

Session 4: 'Generation Rising'
taken from the album *Take Back the Beat* by The Tribe
(Alliance Music, 2001)

Session 5: 'Live for You'
taken from the album *Live for You* by Rachael Lampa
(Word Entertainment, 2000)

Session 6: 'Unforgetful You'
taken from the album *If I Left the Zoo* by Jars of Clay
(Essential, 1999)

Session 7: 'Treasure'
taken from the album *The River Flows* by Iona
(Open Sky, 2002)

Session 8: 'Be Thou My Vision'
taken from the album *The Breaking of the Dawn* by Fernando Ortega
(Word Entertainment, 1998)

Session 9: 'There is a Day'
taken from the album *Heavenbound* by Phatfish
(Word Entertainment, 2001)

Session 10: 'The Cross'
taken from the album *Heavenbound* by Phatfish
(Word Entertainment, 2001)

INTRODUCTION

Stop for a moment and listen. What do you hear? Listen harder. Now listen with your inner, spiritual ears. What do you hear? Anything different?

Jesus listened on two levels. He listened to what was going on around him, to the people and the activity, but he also listened to his father. And the two were often tied together.

These devotional sessions provide an opportunity to listen on two levels – to focus your mind on listening to Jesus through his word while also listening to contemporary music.

This book contains two sets of sessions: There are 10 devotional sessions written for young people. These will work best when done alone and in a relaxed environment. There are also 10 sessions for youth leaders. These are meant to be done in a group context.

Each devotional session has a youth group session which ties into it and picks up on the same theme.

The impact of the book will be maximised when devotional sessions and group sessions are done in tandem with young people looking at a devotional session in the week and the youth leader using the related group session at the next group meeting.

The discipline of regularly carving out a time alone with God can be hard. Many young people struggle with it – not because it's time with God, but because the traditional model of silent prayer and a scripture portion is about as appealing as a maths exam. The approach used here tries to bring God's word to life through sound, not silence.

This book ties together Bible study, prayer and contemplation in a youth-friendly format. It uses some fantastic contemporary Christian music, a youth translation of the Bible and plenty of innovative ideas.

Youth leaders should consider providing personal copies of the book for each member of their group. They can then make notes in their copy, and bring it to the group meetings. Youth workers could also consider asking one, or several of the group, to prepare a five-minute presentation for the group based on what they have learnt in their devotional study.

Enjoy hearing the word through sound . . .

YOUNG PEOPLE'S TIME WITH GOD

1. GOD WITH US

TRACK 1 : **'PARALYZED'** BY SIXPENCE NONE THE RICHER

 PASSAGE: MATTHEW 1 & 2
SECTIONS TO BE READ: MATTHEW 1:18–2:23

1 The Family History of Jesus

¹ This is the family history of Jesus Christ. He came from the family of David, and David came from the family of Abraham.

² Abraham was the father of Isaac.
Isaac was the father of Jacob.
Jacob was the father of Judah and his brothers.

³ Judah was the father of Perez and Zerah.
(Their mother was Tamar.)
Perez was the father of Hezron.
Hezron was the father of Ram.

⁴ Ram was the father of Amminadab.
Amminadab was the father of Nahshon.
Nahshon was the father of Salmon.

⁵ Salmon was the father of Boaz.
(Boaz's mother was Rahab.)
Boaz was the father of Obed.
(Obed's mother was Ruth.)
Obed was the father of Jesse.

⁶ Jesse was the father of King David.
David was the father of Solomon.
(Solomon's mother had been Uriah's wife.)

⁷ Solomon was the father of Rehoboam.
Rehoboam was the father of Abijah.
Abijah was the father of Asa.

⁸ Asa was the father of Jehoshaphat.
Jehoshaphat was the father of Jehoram.
Jehoram was the ancestor of Uzziah.

⁹ Uzziah was the father of Jotham.
Jotham was the father of Ahaz.
Ahaz was the father of Hezekiah.

¹⁰ Hezekiah was the father of Manasseh.
Manasseh was the father of Amon.
Amon was the father of Josiah.

¹¹ Josiah was the grandfather of Jehoiachin and his brothers.
(This was at the time that the people were taken to Babylon.)

[12] After they were taken to Babylon:
Jehoiachin was the father of Shealtiel.
Shealtiel was the grandfather of Zerubbabel.

[13] Zerubbabel was the father of Abiud.
Abiud was the father of Eliakim.
Eliakim was the father of Azor.

[14] Azor was the father of Zadok.
Zadok was the father of Akim.
Akim was the father of Eliud.

[15] Eliud was the father of Eleazar.
Eleazar was the father of Matthan.
Matthan was the father of Jacob.

[16] Jacob was the father of Joseph.
Joseph was the husband of Mary,
and Mary was the mother of Jesus.
Jesus is called the Christ.

[17] So there were fourteen generations from Abraham to David. And there were fourteen generations from David until the people were taken to Babylon. And there were fourteen generations from the time when the people were taken to Babylon until Christ was born.

The Birth of Jesus Christ

[18] This is how the birth of Jesus Christ came about. His mother Mary was engaged to marry Joseph, but before they married, she learned she was pregnant by the power of the Holy Spirit. [19] Because Mary's husband, Joseph, was a good man, he did not want to disgrace her in public, so he planned to divorce her secretly.

[20] While Joseph thought about these things, an angel of the Lord came to him in a dream. The angel said, 'Joseph, descendant of David, don't be afraid to take Mary as your wife, because the baby in her is from the Holy Spirit. [21] She will give birth to a son, and you will name him Jesus, because he will save his people from their sins.'

[22] All this happened to bring about what the Lord had said through the prophet: [23]'The virgin will be pregnant. She will have a son, and they will name him Immanuel,' which means 'God is with us'.

[24] When Joseph woke up, he did what the Lord's angel had told him to do. Joseph took Mary as his wife, [25] but he did not have sexual relations with her until she gave birth to the son. And Joseph named him Jesus.

2 Wise Men Come to Visit Jesus

[1] Jesus was born in the town of Bethlehem in Judea during the time when Herod was king. When Jesus was born, some wise men from the east came to Jerusalem. [2] They asked, 'Where is the baby who was born to be the king of the Jews? We saw his star in the east and have come to worship him.'

[3] When King Herod heard this, he was troubled, as well as all the people in Jerusalem. [4] Herod called a meeting of all the leading priests and teachers of the law and asked them where the Christ would be born. [5] They answered, 'In the town of Bethlehem in Judea. The prophet wrote about this in the Scriptures:

[6] "But you, Bethlehem, in the land of Judah,
are important among the tribes of Judah.
A ruler will come from you
who will be like a shepherd for my people Israel.'"   *Micah 5:2*

[7] Then Herod had a secret meeting with the wise men and learned from them the exact time they first saw the star. [8] He sent the wise men to Bethlehem, saying, 'Look carefully for the child. When you find him, come tell me so I can worship him too.'

[9] After the wise men heard the king, they left. The star that they had seen in the east went before them until it stopped above the place where the child was. [10] When the wise men saw the star, they were filled with joy. [11] They came to the house where the child was and saw him with his mother, Mary, and they bowed down and worshiped him. They opened their gifts and gave him treasures of gold, frankincense and myrrh. [12] But God warned the wise men in a dream not to go back to Herod, so they returned to their own country by a different way.

Jesus' Parents Take Him to Egypt

[13] After they left, an angel of the Lord came to Joseph in a dream and said, 'Get up! Take the child and his mother and escape to Egypt, because Herod is starting to look for the child so he can kill him. Stay in Egypt until I tell you to return.'

[14] So Joseph got up and left for Egypt during the night with the child and his mother. [15] And Joseph stayed in Egypt until Herod died. This happened to bring about what the Lord had said through the prophet: 'I called my son out of Egypt.'

Herod Kills the Baby Boys

[16] When Herod saw that the wise men had tricked him, he was furious. So he gave an order to kill all the baby boys in Bethlehem and in the surrounding area who were two years old or younger. This was in keeping with the time he learnt from the wise men. [17] So what God had said through the prophet Jeremiah came true:

[18] 'A voice was heard in Ramah
of painful crying and deep sadness:
Rachel crying for her children.
She refused to be comforted,
because her children are dead.'   *Jeremiah 31:15*

Joseph and Mary Return

[19] After Herod died, an angel of the Lord spoke to Joseph in a dream while he was in Egypt. [20] The angel said, 'Get up! Take the child and his mother and go to the land of Israel, because the people who were trying to kill the child are now dead.'

[21] So Joseph took the child and his mother and went to Israel. [22] But he heard that Archelaus was now king in Judea since his father Herod had died. So Joseph was afraid to go there. After being warned in a dream, he went to the area of Galilee, [23] to a town called Nazareth, and lived there. And so what God had said through the prophets came true: 'He will be called a Nazarene.'

Read Matthew 1:18–2:23

The process of Jesus coming to earth was no stroll in the park. If you'd been around at the time and read about it in the local paper you'd never have believed it. It might have read something like this:

'MIRACLE BABY' ROW FUELS FEAR OF GENOCIDE

Controversy has been sparked after a young woman claimed to have conceived a baby while still a virgin.

The woman's fiancé, who stood by her, says he received a visit from an angel advising him that the embryo was divine.

After the child was born on 25 December, the situation was further complicated when several astrologers arrived claiming to have followed a star. They believe it appeared in the sky marking the boy's location.

Gifts including gold were delivered to the low-income family, who are currently being housed in a shed type structure.

Concern is growing among Israel's ruling elite after advisors warned of widespread political consequences. There are fears that a systematic genocide of all boys in Bethlehem is being planned to eradicate the child whose exact whereabouts are unknown.

The boy's adopted father, known only as Joseph, is confident, however, that the child will not be harmed. He believes an angel regularly warns him of danger.

Sources close to the country's leaders have confirmed that the boy's appearance is causing concern. Historians who are following the case believe the baby's life matches predictions in ancient manuscripts about a promised 'people's leader'.

THE JESUS ASSASSINATION PLOT

Take a look at the following verses:

- Matthew 2:13
- Matthew 2:16–18

It seems crazy that Jesus, the one sent to show a way out of violence, insecurity and death was nearly murdered before his second birthday!

LISTEN TO THE TRACK > > > > >

'**Paralyzed**' refers to bloodshed, death, war and grief. The sorts of things you've just read about. It sums up why Jesus had to come.

After listening, get hold of any newspaper and look through it. What are the stories about? Does it feel like God's saving power is still needed?

LISTEN TO THE TRACK AGAIN > > > > >

As you listen to the situations, think about the fact that the name Jesus means 'God Saves' and that there is hope in all situations because Jesus came.

PARALYSED?

The track you listened to is entitled 'Paralyzed'. It is about feeling powerless when faced with a society that is so against what God wants. Do you relate to this? Have you ever felt 'paralysed' and unable to see how living God's way can make a difference?

God's prophet Elijah felt paralysed with fear after he tried to turn the people of Israel back to God. The Bible says, 'Elijah was afraid and ran for his life . . . He came to a broom tree, sat down under it and prayed that he might die. "I have had enough Lord," he said, "Take my life"' (1 Kings 19:4, NIV).

God came to earth because he knew that even the strongest, most committed prophet or disciple was not strong enough to bring change in the face of the wickedness on earth.

Read Matthew 1:20–21. Let it sink in. This verse isn't just announcing what Jesus would do; it's announcing what we, as humans, can't do. If we could change things on our own, Jesus wouldn't have needed to come.

Refer back to the newspaper you looked through. Many of the reports probably relate to acts of violence, selfishness, anger, greed and even murder. Does this mean that Jesus didn't have much of an impact on society?

Read Matthew 1:23 and Matthew 2:6. Jesus is described not as a police officer or a social worker. He's described as a shepherd – a leader of people. His mission wasn't to clean up the earth, but to empower his followers so that they didn't feel paralysed and could change the world.

As you listen, think about the fact that Jesus is 'Immanuel' – God with us. Try to identify one area you want God to empower you in and spend time reflecting on God's power to do this. Use Matthew 5:16 to focus your prayers.

THE INCARNATION

Theologians describe what Jesus did by coming to earth in human form as 'the incarnation'. The term 'incarnational ministry' is sometimes used to describe a style of Christian ministry which involves moving into an area to work alongside and help people – like Jesus did when he moved from heaven to earth.

THOUGHTS AND THINGS GOD SAID

2. TEMPTATION

TRACK 2: **'STILL BURNING'** BY SIXPENCE NONE THE RICHER

✝ **PASSAGE: MATTHEW 3 & 4**
SECTIONS TO BE READ: MATTHEW 3:13–17 AND 4:1–25.

3 The Work of John the Baptist

¹About that time John the Baptist began preaching in the desert area of Judea. ² John said, 'Change your hearts and lives because the kingdom of heaven is near.' ³ John the Baptist is the one Isaiah the prophet was talking about when he said:

'This is a voice of one
who calls out in the desert:
"Prepare the way for the Lord.
Make the road straight for him."'   *Isaiah 40:3*

⁴John's clothes were made from camel's hair, and he wore a leather belt around his waist. For food, he ate locusts and wild honey. ⁵Many people came from Jerusalem and Judea and all the area around the Jordan River to hear John. ⁶They confessed their sins, and he baptised them in the Jordan River.

⁷Many of the Pharisees and Sadducees came to the place where John was baptising people. When John saw them, he said, 'You are all snakes! Who warned you to run away from God's coming punishment? ⁸Do the things that show you really have changed your hearts and lives. ⁹And don't think you can say to yourselves, "Abraham is our father." I tell you that God could make children for Abraham from these rocks. ¹⁰The axe is now ready to cut down the trees, and every tree that does not produce good fruit will be cut down and thrown into the fire.

¹¹'I baptise you with water to show that your hearts and lives have changed. But there is one coming after me who is greater than I am, whose sandals I am not good enough to carry. He will baptise you with the Holy Spirit and fire. ¹²He will come ready to clean the grain, separating the good grain from the chaff. He will put the good part of the grain into his barn, but he will burn the chaff with a fire that cannot be put out.'

Jesus Is Baptised by John

¹³ At that time Jesus came from Galilee to the Jordan River and wanted John to baptise him. ¹⁴ But John tried to stop him, saying, 'Why do you come to me to be baptised? I need to be baptised by you!'

¹⁵ Jesus answered, 'Let it be this way for now. We should do all things that are God's will.' So John agreed to baptise Jesus.

¹⁶ As soon as Jesus was baptised, he came up out of the water. Then heaven opened, and he saw God's Spirit coming down on him like a dove. ¹⁷ And a voice from heaven said, 'This is my Son, whom I love, and I am very pleased with him.'

17

4 The Temptation of Jesus

¹Then the Spirit led Jesus into the desert to be tempted by the devil. ²Jesus ate nothing for 40 days and nights. After this, he was very hungry. ³The devil came to Jesus to tempt him, saying, 'If you are the Son of God, tell these rocks to become bread.'

⁴Jesus answered, 'It is written in the Scriptures, "A person does not live by eating only bread, but by everything God says."'

⁵Then the devil led Jesus to the holy city of Jerusalem and put him on a high place of the Temple. ⁶The devil said, 'If you are the Son of God, jump down, because it is written in the Scriptures:

"He has put his angels in charge of you.
They will catch you in their hands
so that you will not hit your foot on a rock."'   *Psalm 91:11-12*

⁷Jesus answered him, 'It also says in the Scriptures, "Do not test the Lord your God."'

⁸Then the devil led Jesus to the top of a very high mountain and showed him all the kingdoms of the world and all their splendor. ⁹The devil said, 'If you will bow down and worship me, I will give you all these things.'

¹⁰Jesus said to the devil, 'Go away from me, Satan! It is written in the Scriptures, "You must worship the Lord your God and serve only him."'

¹¹So the devil left Jesus, and angels came and took care of him.

Jesus Begins Work in Galilee

¹²When Jesus heard that John had been put in prison, he went back to Galilee. ¹³He left Nazareth and went to live in Capernaum, a town near Lake Galilee, in the area near Zebulun and Naphtali. ¹⁴Jesus did this to bring about what the prophet Isaiah had said:

¹⁵'Land of Zebulun and land of Naphtali
along the sea,
beyond the Jordan River.
This is Galilee where the non-Jewish people live.

¹⁶These people who live in darkness
will see a great light.
They live in a place covered with the shadows of death,
but a light will shine on them.'   *Isaiah 9:1-2*

Jesus Chooses Some Followers

¹⁷From that time Jesus began to preach, saying, 'Change your hearts and lives, because the kingdom of heaven is near.'

¹⁸As Jesus was walking by Lake Galilee, he saw two brothers, Simon (called Peter) and his brother Andrew. They were throwing a net into the lake because they were fishermen. ¹⁹Jesus said, 'Come follow me, and I will make you fish for people.' ²⁰So Simon and Andrew immediately left their nets and followed him.

²¹As Jesus continued walking by Lake Galilee, he saw two other brothers, James and John, the sons of Zebedee. They were in a boat with their father Zebedee, mending their nets. Jesus told them to come with him. ²²Immediately they left the boat and their father, and they followed Jesus.

Jesus Teaches and Heals People

²³ Jesus went everywhere in Galilee, teaching in the synagogues, preaching the Good News about the kingdom of heaven, and healing all the people's diseases and sicknesses. ²⁴ The news about Jesus spread all over Syria, and people brought all the sick to him. They were suffering from different kinds of diseases. Some were in great pain, some had demons, some were epileptics, and some were paralysed. Jesus healed all of them. ²⁵ Many people from Galilee, the Ten Towns, Jerusalem, Judea and the land across the Jordan River followed him.

Read Matthew 3:13–17 and Matthew 4:1–25.

Note that it was the Holy Spirit who led Jesus to be tempted (4:1). Why do you think God wanted Jesus to go through this?

This track answers the question.

LISTEN TO THE TRACK > > > > >

The key to temptations and hard times is that they are God's arenas for growing us. The song puts it this way: 'The hand that is breaking is that hand that is making all the dead things in me grow . . . So when you break my arms I'll take hold of you.'

In the passage things happened in this order:

- Jesus receives the Holy Spirit after being baptised (3:16).
- God says he loves Jesus and is pleased with him (3:17).
- The Holy Spirit immediately leads Jesus into the desert where, for well over a month, he is tested and tried by the Devil (4:1).
- Jesus is helped by angels after the Devil leaves. He then begins the work God sent him to do (4:17).

Think about this for a few minutes. Usually we expect to be on a high after we've met with God. Usually, after a rough patch, the last thing we think of doing is God's work. What does the order of events, above, tell you? Think on it – it seems that God uses difficult times and temptations as tools to develop us.

THE TEMPTATION

Matthew 4:1–11 shows Jesus being tempted. But did he really need to go through it?

Could he really have been tempted by the thought of owning all the kingdoms of the world? He was God – he created the whole world! It's easy to assume Jesus wasn't really tempted by what the Devil offered – but he was. Think about it:

- **The Devil doesn't mess about – he had everything to play for.** This was his only chance in all eternity to try and get one over on God. He played his best cards and picked things he knew would be attractive to Jesus' human side.
- **The Bible describes it as a test or 'temptation'.** Put another way, Jesus did feel pulled in both directions and could have failed. He had to resist things which 'tempted' and 'enticed' him – it wasn't a forgone conclusion.
- **Jesus avoided food for a whole month and a half** during the temptation to help him focus and be as strong as he could for the test.
- **The Holy Spirit led him into it.** There must have therefore been a reason for it.

THE REASON

Have you ever been through training to learn a new job, skill, craft, or sport? Why did you train? What were the consequences if you messed up the training? What was the point of the training?

Jesus' '40 days' were his training. And when he 'passed', he went straight to Galilee, picked some disciples and kicked off his new job – his ministry (Matthew 4:17).

JESUS' FORMULA

So how did Jesus do it? Resisting temptation and coming through a tough test still smiling is very, very difficult. But Jesus had a secret 'formula' . . .

Find a piece of paper – any size. Write the word 'Temptations' on it and fold it in half, and half again. Do it eight times – then read on.

Your strength has nothing to do with the fact you can't fold the paper more than six times . . . it's impossible. Temptation is like that. However strong, focused or determined we are, we're not strong enough to beat it alone. Jesus wasn't either.

Look at Matthew 4:4, 6 & 7. How did Jesus respond to the temptations? The answer is in the song you listened to: 'So when you break my arms I'll take hold of you'.

The more Jesus was tested the more he looked for God to bring him through it.

Keep the paper as a reminder that your own strength is not enough when you face temptation.

LISTEN TO THE TRACK AGAIN > > > > >

As you listen, acknowledge your own weakness to God, and ask him to be your strength when you face hard times.

> *Jesus had spent time memorising the bits of the Bible which showed what God thought about things like material possessions. He used these to remind both himself and the Devil when he was tempted.*

THOUGHTS AND THINGS GOD SAID

_____

_____

_____

_____

_____

_____

_____

_____

_____

_____

3. SEXUAL PRESSURE

TRACK 3: **'YOU DON'T HAVE TO'** BY THE TRIBE

 PASSAGE: MATTHEW 5
SECTION TO BE READ: MATTHEW 5:1–32

5 Jesus Teaches the People

[1] When Jesus saw the crowds, he went up on a hill and sat down. His followers came to him, [2] and he began to teach them, saying:

[3] 'Those people who know they have great spiritual needs are happy, because the kingdom of heaven belongs to them.

[4] Those who are sad now are happy, because God will comfort them.

[5] Those who are humble are happy, because the earth will belong to them.

[6] Those who want to do right more than anything else are happy, because God will fully satisfy them.

[7] Those who show mercy to others are happy, because God will show mercy to them.

[8] Those who are pure in their thinking are happy, because they will be with God.

[9] Those who work to bring peace are happy, because God will call them his children.

[10] Those who are treated badly for doing good are happy, because the kingdom of heaven belongs to them.

[11] 'People will insult you and hurt you. They will lie and say all kinds of evil things about you because you follow me. But when they do, you will be happy. [12] Rejoice and be glad, because you have a great reward waiting for you in heaven. People did the same evil things to the prophets who lived before you.

You are like Salt and Light

[13] 'You are the salt of the earth. But if the salt loses its salty taste, it cannot be made salty again. It is good for nothing, except to be thrown out and walked on.

[14] 'You are the light that gives light to the world. A city that is built on a hill cannot be hidden. [15] And people don't hide a light under a bowl. They put it on a lampstand so the light shines for all the people in the house. [16] In the same way, you should be a light for other people. Live so that they will see the good things you do and will praise your Father in heaven.

The Importance of the Law

¹⁷ 'Don't think that I have come to destroy the law of Moses or the teaching of the prophets. I have not come to destroy them but to bring about what they said. ¹⁸ I tell you the truth, nothing will disappear from the law until heaven and earth are gone. Not even the smallest letter or the smallest part of a letter will be lost until everything has happened. ¹⁹ Whoever refuses to obey any command and teaches other people not to obey that command will be the least important in the kingdom of heaven. But whoever obeys the commands and teaches other people to obey them will be great in the kingdom of heaven. ²⁰ I tell you that if you are no more obedient than the teachers of the law and the Pharisees, you will never enter the kingdom of heaven.

Jesus Teaches About Anger

²¹ 'You have heard that it was said to our people long ago, "You must not murder anyone. Anyone who murders another will be judged." ²² But I tell you, if you are angry with a brother or sister, you will be judged. If you say bad things to a brother or sister, you will be judged by the council. And if you call someone a fool, you will be in danger of the fire of hell.

²³ 'So when you offer your gift to God at the altar, and you remember that your brother or sister has something against you, ²⁴ leave your gift there at the altar. Go and make peace with that person, and then come and offer your gift.

²⁵ 'If your enemy is taking you to court, become friends quickly, before you go to court. Otherwise, your enemy might turn you over to the judge, and the judge might give you to a guard to put you in jail. ²⁶ I tell you the truth, you will not leave there until you have paid everything you owe.

Jesus Teaches About Sexual Sin

²⁷ 'You have heard that it was said, "You must not be guilty of adultery." ²⁸ But I tell you that if anyone looks at a woman and wants to sin sexually with her, in his mind he has already done that sin with the woman. ²⁹ If your right eye causes you to sin, take it out and throw it away. It is better to lose one part of your body than to have your whole body thrown into hell. ³⁰ If your right hand causes you to sin, cut it off and throw it away. It is better to lose one part of your body than for your whole body to go into hell.

Jesus Teaches About Divorce

³¹ 'It was also said, "Anyone who divorces his wife must give her a written divorce paper." ³² But I tell you that anyone who divorces his wife forces her to be guilty of adultery. The only reason for a man to divorce his wife is if she has sexual relations with another man. And anyone who marries that divorced woman is guilty of adultery.

Make Promises Carefully

³³ 'You have heard that it was said to our people long ago, "Don't break your promises, but keep the promises you make to the Lord." ³⁴ But I tell you, never swear an oath. Don't swear an oath using the name of heaven, because heaven is God's

throne. ³⁵Don't swear an oath using the name of the earth, because the earth belongs to God. Don't swear an oath using the name of Jerusalem, because that is the city of the great King. ³⁶ Don't even swear by your own head, because you cannot make one hair on your head become white or black. ³⁷ Say only yes if you mean yes, and no if you mean no. If you say more than yes or no, it is from the Evil One.

Don't Fight Back

³⁸ 'You have heard that it was said, "An eye for an eye, and a tooth for a tooth." ³⁹ But I tell you, don't stand up against an evil person. If someone slaps you on the right cheek, turn to him the other cheek as well. ⁴⁰ If someone wants to sue you in court and take your shirt, let him have your coat as well. ⁴¹ If someone forces you to go with him a kilometre, go with him 2 kilometres. ⁴² If a person asks you for something, give it to him. Don't refuse to give to someone who wants to borrow from you.

Love All People

⁴³ 'You have heard that it was said, "Love your neighbour and hate your enemies." ⁴⁴ But I say to you, love your enemies. Pray for those who hurt you. ⁴⁵ If you do this, you will be true children of your Father in heaven. He causes the sun to rise on good people and on evil people, and he sends rain to those who do right and to those who do wrong. ⁴⁶ If you love only the people who love you, you will get no reward. Even the tax collectors do that. ⁴⁷ And if you are nice only to your friends, you are no better than other people. Even those who don't know God are nice to their friends. ⁴⁸ So you must be perfect, just as your Father in heaven is perfect.'

Do you ever feel pressured to say certain 'acceptable' things when your peers talk about subjects like girl or boyfriends, sex, where you went at the weekend or what you enjoy doing in your spare time?

The disciples faced exactly the same pressures and Jesus talks to them about it in Matthew 5:1–32.

Read Matthew 5:1–32

Think honestly about which of these makes you happier:

    a. Feeling accepted by your peers
    b. Being true to what you really believe
    c. Feeling you're doing things God's way

If you answered a. then you're not that different from the disciples. Even after spending several years with Jesus, Peter still said what he thought people wanted to hear rather than being true to what he believed deep down, or to what God wanted. Read the story in Matthew 26:69–75.

RADICAL JESUS?

Have you ever heard anyone describe Jesus as a radical? Do you think of Jesus as someone whose ideas and teachings were revolutionary and ground breaking, or do you imagine him as a bearded figure, dressed in white, roaming the fields talking about lost sheep?

The passage you read in Matthew 5 was radical when Jesus first said it, and still is today. Look at the following verses. Imagine you talked to your peers about these and lived them out. What reaction might you get?

- Matthew 5:8
- Matthew 5:13
- Matthew 5:22
- Matthew 5:27

Get some salt. Put it on your tongue and sit for a few minutes while its flavour hits you. Salt is like these ideas. They're so radical that they're not meant to be easy to swallow. But they are meant to make people sit up and listen.

LISTEN TO THE TRACK > > > > >

Whether you're still looking forward to your first kiss, have lost your virginity, or are somewhere in the middle, this does apply to you. Look again at Matthew 5:27–30 where Jesus talks about sexual sin. This is radical. According to his teaching even people who have never had a kiss can be guilty of sexual sin – in their thought life.

SLIDING INTO SIN

Sexual sin is like a slide. Once you climb onto the slide, either in your mind and thoughts, or physically with your partner, it's very hard to stop yourself.

Spend some time reviewing your own thought life and physical dealings in this area. Then meditate on the track lyrics and Bible verses below:

1. God's Flavour
'Those lies will put your lights out.' [The Tribe]
'You are the salt of the earth. If the salt loses its salty taste, it cannot be made salty again.' [Jesus]

2. Obey Who?
'You don't have to when people say [you] do.' [The Tribe]
'Those who want to do right more than anything else are happy, because God will fully satisfy them.' [Jesus]

3. Sexual Sin

'Sex be a sacred thang. Respect this God thang.' [The Tribe]

'If anyone looks at a woman and wants to sin sexually with her, in his mind he has already done that sin with the woman.' [Jesus]

4. Your Identity

'It's question time. Do you know who you are?' [The Tribe]

'You are the light that gives light to the world.' [Jesus]

5. Staying True

'Break out the box, you know you gotta stay true.' [The Tribe]

'Those who are pure in their thinking are happy because they will be with God.' [Jesus]

ACTION PLAN

Pick whichever of the five categories above seem most relevant to you. Commit to do/pray the following four things each day for the next week around the issue you picked:

1. Be 100 per cent honest with God about what you really think about this and talk to him about it.

2. Offer God this area of your life. Ask him to speak to you about it. Spend time listening to God for his answers.

3. Make a list of reasons 'why' (from what God shows you and what you read in Matthew) you need to work on this area.

4. Commit to put into action what God shows you – and think about practical ways you can do this.

THOUGHTS AND THINGS GOD SAID

_____

_____

_____

_____

_____

_____

_____

_____

_____

---

4. THE KINGDOM OF GOD

TRACK 4: **'GENERATION RISING'** BY THE TRIBE

> ✝ **PASSAGE: MATTHEW 13**
> SECTION TO BE READ: MATTHEW 13:1–58

13 A Story About Planting Seed

¹ That same day Jesus went out of the house and sat by the lake. ² Large crowds gathered around him, so he got into a boat and sat down, while the people stood on the shore. ³ Then Jesus used stories to teach them many things. He said: 'A farmer went out to plant his seed. ⁴ While he was planting, some seed fell by the road, and the birds came and ate it all up. ⁵ Some seed fell on rocky ground, where there wasn't much earth. That seed grew very fast, because the ground was not deep. ⁶ But when the sun rose, the plants dried up, because they did not have deep roots. ⁷ Some other seed fell among thorny weeds, which grew and choked the good plants. ⁸ Some other seed fell on good ground where it grew and produced a crop. Some plants made 100 times more, some made 60 times more, and some made 30 times more. ⁹ You people who can hear me, listen.'

Why Jesus Used Stories to Teach

¹⁰ The followers came to Jesus and asked, 'Why do you use stories to teach the people?'

¹¹ Jesus answered, 'You have been chosen to know the secrets about the kingdom of heaven, but others cannot know these secrets. ¹² Those who have understanding will be given more, and they will have all they need. But those who do not have understanding, even what they have will be taken away from them. ¹³ This is why I use stories to teach the people: they see, but they don't really see. They hear, but they don't really hear or understand. ¹⁴ So they show that the things Isaiah said about them are true:
'You will listen and listen, but you will not understand.
You will look and look, but you will not learn.

¹⁵ For the minds of these people have become stubborn.
They do not hear with their ears,
and they have closed their eyes.
Otherwise they might really understand
what they see with their eyes
and hear with their ears.
They might really understand in their minds
and come back to me and be healed.'   *Isaiah 6:9–10*

[16] But you are blessed, because you see with your eyes and hear with your ears. [17] I tell you the truth, many prophets and good people wanted to see the things that you now see, but they did not see them. And they wanted to hear the things that you now hear, but they did not hear them.

Jesus Explains the Seed Story

[18] 'So listen to the meaning of that story about the farmer. [19] What is the seed that fell by the road? That seed is like the person who hears the message about the kingdom but does not understand it. The Evil One comes and takes away what was planted in that person's heart. [20] And what is the seed that fell on rocky ground? That seed is like the person who hears the teaching and quickly accepts it with joy. [21] But he does not let the teaching go deep into his life, so he keeps it only a short time. When trouble or persecution comes because of the teaching he accepted, he quickly gives up. [22] And what is the seed that fell among the thorny weeds? That seed is like the person who hears the teaching but lets worries about this life and the temptation of wealth stop that teaching from growing. So the teaching does not produce fruit in that person's life. [23] But what is the seed that fell on the good ground? That seed is like the person who hears the teaching and understands it. That person grows and produces fruit, sometimes 100 times more, sometimes 60 times more, and sometimes 30 times more.'

A Story About Wheat and Weeds

[24] Then Jesus told them another story: 'The kingdom of heaven is like a man who planted good seed in his field. [25] That night, when everyone was asleep, his enemy came and planted weeds among the wheat and then left. [26] Later, the wheat grew and the heads of grain grew, but the weeds also grew. [27] Then the man's servants came to him and said, "You planted good seed in your field. Where did the weeds come from?" [28] The man answered, "An enemy planted weeds." The servants asked, "Do you want us to pull up the weeds?" [29] The man answered, "No, because when you pull up the weeds, you might also pull up the wheat. [30] Let the weeds and the wheat grow together until the harvest time. At harvest time I will tell the workers, 'First gather the weeds and tie them together to be burnt. Then gather the wheat and bring it to my barn.'"'

Stories of Mustard Seed and Yeast

[31] Then Jesus told another story: 'The kingdom of heaven is like a mustard seed that a man planted in his field. [32] That seed is the smallest of all seeds, but when it grows, it is one of the largest garden plants. It becomes big enough for the wild birds to come and build nests in its branches.'

[33] Then Jesus told another story: 'The kingdom of heaven is like yeast that a woman took and hid in a large bowl of flour until it made all the dough rise.'

[34] Jesus used stories to tell all these things to the people; he always used stories to teach them. [35] This is as the prophet said:
'I will speak using stories;
I will tell things that have been secret since the world was made.'   *Psalm 78:2*

Jesus Explains About the Weeds

36 Then Jesus left the crowd and went into the house. His followers came to him and said, 'Explain to us the meaning of the story about the weeds in the field.'

37 Jesus answered, 'The man who planted the good seed in the field is the Son of Man. 38 The field is the world, and the good seeds are all of God's children who belong to the kingdom. The weeds are those people who belong to the Evil One. 39 And the enemy who planted the bad seed is the devil. The harvest time is the end of the world, and the workers who gather are God's angels.

40 'Just as the weeds are pulled up and burnt in the fire, so it will be at the end of the world. 41 The Son of Man will send out his angels, and they will gather out of his kingdom all who cause sin and all who do evil. 42 The angels will throw them into the blazing furnace, where the people will cry and grind their teeth with pain. 43 Then the good people will shine like the sun in the kingdom of their Father. You people who can hear me, listen.

Stories of a Treasure and a Pearl

44 'The kingdom of heaven is like a treasure hidden in a field. One day a man found the treasure, and then he hid it in the field again. He was so happy that he went and sold everything he owned to buy that field.

45 'Also, the kingdom of heaven is like a man looking for fine pearls. 46 When he found a very valuable pearl, he went and sold everything he had and bought it.

A Story of a Fishing Net

47 'Also, the kingdom of heaven is like a net that was put into the lake and caught many different kinds of fish. 48 When it was full, the fishermen pulled the net to the shore. They sat down and put all the good fish in baskets and threw away the bad fish. 49 It will be this way at the end of the world. The angels will come and separate the evil people from the good people. 50 The angels will throw the evil people into the blazing furnace, where people will cry and grind their teeth with pain.'

51 Jesus asked his followers, 'Do you understand all these things?'
They answered, 'Yes, we understand.'

52 Then Jesus said to them, 'So every teacher of the law who has been taught about the kingdom of heaven is like the owner of a house. He brings out both new things and old things he has saved.'

Jesus Goes to His Home Town

53 When Jesus finished teaching with these stories, he left there. 54 He went to his home town and taught the people in the synagogue, and they were amazed. They said, 'Where did this man get this wisdom and this power to do miracles? 55 He is just the son of a carpenter. His mother is Mary, and his brothers are James, Joseph, Simon, and Judas. 56 And all his sisters are here with us. Where then does this man get all these things?' 57 So the people were upset with Jesus.

But Jesus said to them, 'A prophet is honoured everywhere except in his home town and in his own home.'

58 So he did not do many miracles there because they had no faith.

What do you think of when you see or hear the words 'The Kingdom of God'? Write down a line describing what you think the Kingdom of God is: _____

The Kingdom of God is hard to define. There are many parts to it. Circle *'Agree'* or *'Disagree'* in the following quiz to explore your understanding of it:

The Kingdom of God . . .

1. . . . is not a real earthly kingdom, it's a spiritual kingdom. *Agree/Disagree*

2. . . . is something Jesus didn't really talk about. *Agree/Disagree*

3. . . . has not yet come. It will come when Jesus returns. *Agree/Disagree*

4. . . . is something only church leaders can see. *Agree/Disagree*

5. . . . is something that all Christians are meant to build. *Agree/Disagree*

6. . . . is as a small as a mustard seed but stretches across the world. *Agree/Disagree*

7. . . . is something Jesus said had arrived. *Agree/Disagree*

8. . . . is located in Jerusalem. *Agree/Disagree*

Now look at the answers: *1. It's spiritual but also impacts the real world. 2. Wrong – Jesus' whole ministry was proclaiming the Kingdom. 3. It has come in part, but will be completed perfectly at the second coming. 4. Wrong – all Christians can see the Kingdom. 5. Yes – all disciples are called to build God's Kingdom. 6. True – it starts in the heart but impacts the world. 7. True – see Matthew 4:17. 8. False – it's located in the hearts of Christians.*

BUT WHAT IS IT?

At its most simple level the Kingdom of God can be described as the 'experience of blessing'. In other words it isn't a kingdom in the way earthly kingdoms are usually defined – through physical factors like location, size, population or wealth. Instead it's located and accessed in the heart. It's a spiritual kingdom, which is defined by the blessing and change it brings.

This doesn't mean though that it's irrelevant 'pie in the sky' nonsense. When Jesus talked about the Kingdom he did so in terms of the real life evidence of it – the acts and signs of God in the world such as the blind seeing, the crippled walking and the good news being preached (see Matthew 11:4–6). So, if we all stopped living out our faith in the gritty reality of life, there would be no Kingdom to show. The Kingdom starts with faith and a vision of the world as Jesus wants it. It grows in our hearts and spills out into situations where God's love is needed.

Think about this for a minute and try to write down in your own words ways in which you have experienced the Kingdom of God in your life and the world around you.

LISTEN TO THE TRACK > > > > >

It's a great vision of what it means to live out the Kingdom. Which parts of the song did you most relate to? Why?

SECRETS OF THE KINGDOM

Jesus talked about the 'secrets of the Kingdom of Heaven' (Matthew 13:11) and revealed them through stories and parables. Look at the parables in this passage and try to uncover the message Jesus was giving about the Kingdom through each one. Make a list of the characteristics of the Kingdom from what you learn:

The Seed parable
What stops the Kingdom becoming rooted in people's lives? (v.21 & 22)

The Weed parable
Are there only good people in God's Kingdom? (v.41)
What effect do people who have accepted the Kingdom have in the world? (v.43)

Mustard Seed and Yeast parable
What does the mustard seed parable say about the influence of the Kingdom? (v.32)
What does the yeast parable show about the influence of the Kingdom? (v.33 – clue: yeast spreads through all the dough)

Treasure and Pearl parable
What does the treasure story say about the effect the Kingdom has on people when they discover it? (v.44)
What does the pearl parable say about what people must give up to find the Kingdom? (v.46)

LISTEN TO THE TRACK AGAIN > > > > >

Keep an ear out for any characteristics of the Kingdom (radical lifestyle, following Jesus' lead etc). It's a good summary of what the Kingdom of God looks like when it's brought to life in our lives – its key message is the Kingdom being brought to life through active discipleship.

The track describes the Kingdom as 'a vision to be held tight and made real'. Using the list you made above, of the characteristics of the Kingdom, write down any situations in your own life or environment in which the Kingdom of God needs to be seen. Think through and talk to God about how you can make the vision of the Kingdom real in these situations.

THOUGHTS AND THINGS GOD SAID

_____

_____

_____

_____

_____

_____

_____

_____

_____

_____

5. FAITH

TRACK 5: **'LIVE FOR YOU'** BY RACHAEL LAMPA

 PASSAGE: MATTHEW 16
SECTION TO BE READ: MATTHEW 16:1–28

5 The Leaders Ask for a Miracle

¹ The Pharisees and Sadducees came to Jesus, wanting to trick him. So they asked him to show them a miracle from God.

² Jesus answered, 'At sunset you say we will have good weather, because the sky is red. ³ And in the morning you say that it will be a rainy day, because the sky is dark and red. You see these signs in the sky and know what they mean. In the same way, you see the things that I am doing now, but you don't know their meaning. ⁴ Evil and sinful people ask for a miracle as a sign, but they will not be given any sign, except the sign of Jonah.' Then Jesus left them and went away.

Guard Against Wrong Teachings

⁵ Jesus' followers went across the lake, but they had forgotten to bring bread. ⁶ Jesus said to them, 'Be careful! Beware of the yeast of the Pharisees and the Sadducees.'

⁷ His followers discussed the meaning of this, saying, 'He said this because we forgot to bring bread.'

⁸ Knowing what they were talking about, Jesus asked them, 'Why are you talking about not having bread? Your faith is small. ⁹ Do you still not understand? Remember the five loaves of bread that fed the 5,000? And remember that you filled many baskets with the leftovers? ¹⁰ Or the seven loaves of bread that fed the 4,000 and the many baskets you then also filled? ¹¹ I was not talking to you about bread. Why don't you understand that? I am telling you to beware of the yeast of the Pharisees and the Sadducees.' ¹² Then the followers understood that Jesus was not telling them to beware of the yeast used in bread but to beware of the teaching of the Pharisees and the Sadducees.

Peter Says Jesus is the Christ

¹³ When Jesus came to the area of Caesarea Philippi, he asked his followers, 'Who do people say the Son of Man is?'

¹⁴ They answered, 'Some say you are John the Baptist. Others say you are Elijah, and still others say you are Jeremiah or one of the prophets.'

¹⁵ Then Jesus asked them, 'And who do you say I am?'

¹⁶ Simon Peter answered, 'You are the Christ, the Son of the living God.'

¹⁷ Jesus answered, 'You are blessed, Simon son of Jonah, because no person taught you

that. My Father in heaven showed you who I am. [18] So I tell you, you are Peter. On this rock I will build my church, and the power of death will not be able to defeat it. [19] I will give you the keys of the kingdom of heaven; the things you don't allow on earth will be the things that God does not allow, and the things you allow on earth will be the things that God allows.' [20] Then Jesus warned his followers not to tell anyone he was the Christ.

Jesus Says that He Must Die

[21] From that time on Jesus began telling his followers that he must go to Jerusalem, where the older Jewish leaders, the leading priests, and the teachers of the law would make him suffer many things. He told them he must be killed and then be raised from the dead on the third day.

[22] Peter took Jesus aside and told him not to talk like that. He said, 'God save you from those things, Lord! Those things will never happen to you!'

[23] Then Jesus said to Peter, 'Go away from me, Satan! You are not helping me! You don't care about the things of God, but only about the things people think are important.'

[24] Then Jesus said to his followers, 'If people want to follow me, they must give up the things they want. They must be willing even to give up their lives to follow me. [25] Those who want to save their lives will give up true life, and those who give up their lives for me will have true life. [26] It is worth nothing for them to have the whole world if they lose their souls. They could never pay enough to buy back their souls. [27] The Son of Man will come again with his Father's glory and with his angels. At that time, he will reward them for what they have done. [28] I tell you the truth, some people standing here will see the Son of Man coming with his kingdom before they die.'

LISTEN TO THE TRACK > > > > >

Open your heart to God. Tell him that you want him to teach you something new, through this devotional, about really living for him.

Read Matthew 16:1–28 and as you do, follow the sections below, in which Jesus reveals some of the features of faith:

1. Matthew 16:1–12: it enables you to see *deeper meaning* in things.
2. Matthew 16:13–20: it comes *from* God.
3. Matthew 16:21–23: it has to be developed, nurtured and grown – it's *not instant*.
4. Matthew 16:24–28: it *enables you* to do things which, from an earthly point of view, make no sense.

Write down below your own definition of faith based on your experiences of living for God. Use the following words to get you thinking:

Supernatural, deep, blind, exciting, draining, hope-inspiring, complicated, costly, God-centred, personal, doubt-filled, demanding, easy.

Faith is _____

STRONG STUFF

Look at the following paraphrases of things Jesus says in the passage. Do they make sense to you?

- 'Following me will involve giving up certain things you desire.' (Matthew 16:24)
- 'The way to find a really fulfilling life is to look in unexpected places. Stop trying to find life through material things. You'll only find it when you give up that search.' (Matthew 16:25)
- 'Compared to your inner centre (or soul), all the possessions you most want are empty. Chasing all those possessions can destroy your soul.' (Matthew 16:26)

These can seem slightly upside down, even crazy. That's because they lack the key ingredient – human faith. The key to the teachings of Jesus in Matthew 16 is faith. Without faith these are the ramblings of a lunatic – and without faith, trying to follow these teachings is mad.

Faith is having enough belief or trust in someone to act on what you know of them. If you have faith in a friend's driving you'll go in their car. If you have faith that God is reliable and dependable then you'll act on what he says – however crazy it might seem.

BLIND FAITH?

So what is blind faith and does anyone live their life by blind faith? The answer is yes – most of us do. Have a look at the following quiz, answering yes or no to each question:

1. Have you ever flown in an aeroplane? *Yes/No*

2. Have you ever been to the optician to have your eyes tested? *Yes/No*

3. Have you been in a taxi? *Yes/No*

4. Have you ever been on large rides at a theme park? *Yes/No*

5. Have you ever been on a ferry or boat? *Yes/No*

6. Have you ever been treated in hospital? *Yes/No*

7. Have you ever been on a train? *Yes/No*

8. Have you ever been to your local doctor for advice? *Yes/No*

9. Have you ever been on a bus? *Yes/No*

10. Have you ever been to the dentist? *Yes/No*

If you answered yes to even one question, then you have acted in blind faith. Assuming you didn't know the doctor or bus driver, you still chose to put your life in their hands. This sort of blind faith isn't what Jesus wants. He wants us to know him so that when we alter our decisions and actions because of him, we can have confidence he isn't going to let us down.

LISTEN TO THE TRACK AGAIN > > > > >

It's a great summary of faith:

- **The first section** refers to how God has shown himself to be faithful: 'You've walked these roads before me. You've known the pain of a broken heart.'
- **The second section** is a response to what God has shown about who he is: 'Help me now to trust you, every single day to follow in your way.'
- **The third section** refers to faith in action and relates to Matthew 16:24: 'Everything I ever thought was mine I give it all away.'

Spend some time evaluating how well you feel you know God. The key to growing your faith is to grow your relationship with God. Re-read Matthew 16, inviting God to reveal things about his character and who he is to you through it. Remember that as your understanding of God and love for him grows, your faith in him will as well.

> *According to Jesus' brother, James, real faith is not about what you believe, but about what you do. The demons believe God is real but it doesn't save them, he says. James wrote that, faith that does nothing is worth nothing and said, ' I will show you my faith by what I do'.*

THOUGHTS AND THINGS GOD SAID

_____
_____
_____
_____
_____
_____
_____
_____
_____
_____

6. BEING TRANSFORMED

TRACK 6: 'UNFORGETFUL YOU' BY JARS OF CLAY

 PASSAGE: MATTHEW 17
SECTION TO BE READ: MATTHEW 17:1–23

17 Jesus Talks with Moses and Elijah

[1] Six days later, Jesus took Peter, James and John, the brother of James, up on a high mountain by themselves. [2] While they watched, Jesus' appearance was changed; his face became bright like the sun, and his clothes became white as light. [3] Then Moses and Elijah appeared to them, talking with Jesus.

[4] Peter said to Jesus, 'Lord, it is good that we are here. If you want, I will put up three tents here – one for you, one for Moses and one for Elijah.'

[5] While Peter was talking, a bright cloud covered them. A voice came from the cloud and said, 'This is my Son, whom I love, and I am very pleased with him. Listen to him!'

[6] When his followers heard the voice, they were so frightened they fell to the ground. [7] But Jesus went to them and touched them and said, 'Stand up. Don't be afraid.'

[8] When they looked up, they saw Jesus was now alone.

[9] As they were coming down the mountain, Jesus commanded them not to tell anyone about what they had seen until the Son of Man had risen from the dead.

[10] Then his followers asked him, 'Why do the teachers of the law say that Elijah must come first?'

[11] Jesus answered, 'They are right to say that Elijah is coming and that he will make everything the way it should be. [12] But I tell you that Elijah has already come, and they did not recognise him. They did to him whatever they wanted to do. It will be the same with the Son of Man; those same people will make the Son of Man suffer.' [13] Then the followers understood that Jesus was talking about John the Baptist.

Jesus Heals a Sick Boy

[14] When Jesus and his followers came back to the crowd, a man came to Jesus and bowed before him. [15] The man said, 'Lord, have mercy on my son. He has epilepsy and is suffering very much, because he often falls into the fire or into the water. [16] I brought him to your followers, but they could not cure him.'

[17] Jesus answered, 'You people have no faith, and your lives are all wrong. How long must I put up with you? How long must I continue to be patient with you? Bring the boy here.' [18] Jesus gave a strong command to the demon inside the boy. Then the demon came out, and the boy was healed from that time on.

[19] The followers came to Jesus when he was alone and asked, 'Why couldn't we force the demon out?'

²⁰ Jesus answered, 'Because your faith is too small. I tell you the truth, if your faith is as big as a mustard seed, you can say to this mountain, 'Move from here to there,' and it will move. All things will be possible for you.' ²¹ 'That kind of spirit comes out only if you use prayer and give up eating.'

Jesus Talks About His Death

²² While Jesus' followers were gathering in Galilee, he said to them, 'The Son of Man will be handed over to people, ²³ and they will kill him. But on the third day he will be raised from the dead.' And the followers were filled with sadness.

Jesus Talks About Paying Taxes

²⁴ When Jesus and his followers came to Capernaum, the men who collected the Temple tax came to Peter. They asked, 'Does your teacher pay the Temple tax?'

²⁵ Peter answered, 'Yes, Jesus pays the tax.'
Peter went into the house, but before he could speak, Jesus said to him, 'What do you think? The kings of the earth collect different kinds of taxes. But who pays the taxes – the king's children or others?'

²⁶ Peter answered, 'Other people pay the taxes.'
Jesus said to Peter, 'Then the children of the king don't have to pay taxes. ²⁷ But we don't want to upset these tax collectors. So go to the lake and fish. After you catch the first fish, open its mouth and you will find a coin. Take that coin and give it to the tax collectors for you and me.'

Read Matthew 17:1–23

You may have been reading this passage wondering what on earth was going on. Before thinking about the theme of change, have a look at the boxes below which explain some of the deeper significance of these events:

WHY DID MOSES AND ELIJAH APPEAR?

Moses was given the law by God in the Old Testament. He represented the old relationship that the Lord had with his people.

Elijah represented the restorer of all things in the Old Testament book of Malachi.

They appeared at the time when Jesus was starting to look ahead to his death. They represented the age passed and the age to come, with Jesus the one who would bring in the new age by dying.

WHY DID PETER WANT TO BUILD SHELTERS?

It wasn't that Peter had been a boy scout and wanted to practise his construction skills, he just wanted the moment to last – something about it made it unforgettable. He thought that building shelters might make Elijah and Moses want to stay. It was usual during the Feast of Tabernacles to build small shelters to stay in.

CHANGE

The symbolism in this passage points to significant changes about to happen. On a more surface level, too, the passage is full of change:

- Jesus' appearance changes (17:2)
- The environment changes – a bright cloud appears (17:5)
- A boy's life is changed – he is healed (17:18)
- Jesus' focus changes – he starts talking about his death (17:22)

Have a glass of water nearby and think about this: if you threw the water up in the air, could you catch it all? If you tried to make it float in the air, could you?

The answer is yes. It just involves changing the water into ice or steam first. And the one thing that causes this change, is the environment the water's in. If the temperature falls below zero, it freezes. If it rises above boiling point it starts to turn into steam. Environment causes change.

ENVIRONMENT

Think about the environments you inhabit and how they affect and change you – in good ways and bad.

LISTEN TO THE TRACK > > > > >

The song is about someone's struggle to change – to become less selfish, to overcome anger and tantrums and to become more aware of God. Make a list of any areas in your own Christian faith in which you struggle to grow and change.

Next to each of these write the environment you're in when you struggle with this. For example, if the struggle is gossip, the environment might be when you are at a certain person's house, or when you are in the company of certain friends.

In the song it's when the singer spends time with God – brings God into the environments he inhabits – that he sees how 'Unforgettable' God is and is influenced to change. It's when he keeps God out that he struggles.

Next to each of the points you've written down, think how it might be different if you talked to and had your thoughts on God in those situations.

Spend some time talking to God about each of the things you want him to help you change and committing to let him be part of those environments.

THOUGHTS AND THINGS GOD SAID

\
\
\
\
\
\
\
\
\
\

7. MATERIALISM

PASSAGE: MATTHEW 19
SECTION TO BE READ: MATTHEW 19:13–30

19 Jesus Teaches About Divorce

¹ After Jesus said all these things, he left Galilee and went into the area of Judea on the other side of the Jordan River. ² Large crowds followed him, and he healed them there.

³ Some Pharisees came to Jesus and tried to trick him. They asked, 'Is it right for a man to divorce his wife for any reason he chooses?'

⁴ Jesus answered, 'Surely you have read in the Scriptures: when God made the world, "he made them male and female". ⁵ And God said, "So a man will leave his father and mother and be united with his wife, and the two will become one body". ⁶ So there are not two, but one. God has joined the two together, so no one should separate them.'

⁷ The Pharisees asked, 'Why then did Moses give a command for a man to divorce his wife by giving her divorce papers?'

⁸ Jesus answered, 'Moses allowed you to divorce your wives because you refused to accept God's teaching, but divorce was not allowed in the beginning. ⁹ I tell you that anyone who divorces his wife and marries another woman is guilty of adultery. The only reason for a man to divorce his wife is if his wife has sexual relations with another man.'

¹⁰ The followers said to him, 'If that is the only reason a man can divorce his wife, it is better not to marry.'

¹¹ Jesus answered, 'Not everyone can accept this teaching, but God has made some able to accept it. ¹² There are different reasons why some men cannot marry. Some men were born without the ability to become fathers. Others were made that way later in life by other people. And some men have given up marriage because of the kingdom of heaven. But the person who can marry should accept this teaching about marriage.'

Jesus Welcomes Children

¹³ Then the people brought their little children to Jesus so he could put his hands on them and pray for them. His followers told them to stop, ¹⁴ but Jesus said, 'Let the little children come to me. Don't stop them, because the kingdom of heaven belongs to people who are like these children.' ¹⁵ After Jesus put his hands on the children, he left that place.

A Rich Young Man's Question

¹⁶ A man came to Jesus and asked, 'Teacher, what good thing must I do to have life for ever?'

[17] Jesus answered, 'Why do you ask me about what is good? Only God is good. But if you want to have life for ever, obey the commands.'

[18] The man asked, 'Which commands?'
Jesus answered, ' "You must not murder anyone; you must not be guilty of adultery; you must not steal; you must not tell lies about your neighbour; [19] honour your father and mother; and love your neighbour as you love yourself." '

[20] The young man said, 'I have obeyed all these things. What else do I need to do?'

[21] Jesus answered, 'If you want to be perfect, then go and sell your possessions and give the money to the poor. If you do this, you will have treasure in heaven. Then come and follow me.'

[22] But when the young man heard this, he left very sad, because he was rich.

[23] Then Jesus said to his followers, 'I tell you the truth, it will be hard for a rich person to enter the kingdom of heaven. [24] Yes, I tell you that it is easier for a camel to go through the eye of a needle than for a rich person to enter the kingdom of God.'

[25] When Jesus' followers heard this, they were very surprised and asked, 'Then who can be saved?'

[26] Jesus looked at them and said, 'This is something people cannot do, but God can do all things.'

[27] Peter said to Jesus, 'Look, we have left everything and followed you. So what will we have?'

[28] Jesus said to them, 'I tell you the truth, when the age to come has arrived, the Son of Man will sit on his great throne. All of you who followed me will also sit on twelve thrones, judging the twelve tribes of Israel. [29] And all those who have left houses, brothers, sisters, father, mother, children or farms to follow me will get much more than they left, and they will have life for ever. [30] Many who have the highest place now will have the lowest place in the future. And many who have the lowest place now will have the highest place in the future.'

LISTEN TO THE TRACK > > > > >

What do you think your treasure is? If you're not sure, think about what makes you come alive, what pulls at your heartstrings, what gives you energy or gets you excited. It might be a vehicle, a mobile phone or palmtop, a piece of clothing, a fast-food outlet, a games console, a band, a club, a range of beauty products – anything.

At this moment, you're probably armouring yourself up against a guilt trip, expecting this session to suggest you reject anything you enjoy and go build a convent on a hill. That won't happen. However, to get the most out of what Jesus has to say about materialism you must be prepared to think honestly. As the following account shows, Jesus never forces anyone to do anything they don't want to . . .

Read Matthew 19:13–30.

Jesus looks at two problems here: materialism and control.

MATERIALISM

Jesus always got specific. In this passage he doesn't talk generally about the masses living in poverty across Israel. He brings it down to this rich young man's front door.

Think:

- Do you get incensed about poverty in developing countries?
- Do you think people and politicians should do more to look after the interests of poor nations, and not just their own?
- Does it get your goat that in the forty seconds it's taken you to read this section, five children have died of preventable diseases? (Christian Aid)

Jesus knew that to get help to the poor, to make society more equal and to prevent the sort of issues listed above he had to strike at the root. He had to talk about our individual approaches to wealth and money. It's very, very easy to think only the government or World Bank can alleviate poverty. But pointing the finger at others can be dangerous . . .

Point your finger at an object near where you are sitting. Amazingly, in doing that, three of your fingers are pointing back at yourself. This is a powerful reminder of the point Jesus is making. It's right to campaign and get vocal about injustices – to point the finger at those who can act but aren't, but only when we're also doing as much, or more ourselves to address the problem.

Read the following true-story which highlights how one person's actions and decision to put their money at God's disposal led to help being given to thousands of marginalized children . . .

THE WALLS' STORY

In 1997, Salvation Army Youth Specialist Phil Wall visited 'Ethembeni', a children's home for AIDS orphans run by the Salvation Army in Southern Africa. Moved with compassion, he and his wife, Wendy, set out to adopt one of the residents – a 2-year-old girl named Zodwa who had lost both her parents to HIV/AIDS.

After nine months of legal constraints their attempt failed. But they were determined to do something and decided that if they could not adopt one child physically, they would raise funds to adopt thousands of AIDS orphans like Zodwa.

Phil and Wendy went about raising funds to start a charity in an unusual way. Using their own savings and money donated by friends, they visited Roots festival, Soul Survivor and several other gatherings. There they presented each delegate with an envelope containing a ten-pound note. The money totalled £5,000. Delegates were challenged to use it to raise further funds, sending the charity what they raised.

Far more money was sent in than had been given out, and the charity HopeHIV was born. Fittingly one of the first major capital projects funded by HopeHIV was the construction of a home for toddlers orphaned by AIDS in Soweto. It was named Zodwa's House. HopeHIV now works in 10 different countries in Africa, making a difference to some of the continent's 12 million orphans.

FEEL POWERLESS?

Very often feelings of powerlessness disable us from doing anything. We see the need, but there's so much of it that we feel inadequate to do anything. Jesus' approach turned this idea on its head. He said the best place to start was doing something small in your own life, before trying to save the whole world. He didn't ask the rich young ruler to end poverty, just to help local poor people.

CONTROL

The account of the rich young ruler has a second message. Jesus reveals that as well as not using his money to help the poor, the rich young man had also allowed his wealth to control him. In other words it could have been the young man's love of anything – cars, food, music, whatever.

All these things, including money, are neutral. The problem is the amount of power they have in our lives. Turn to Matthew 6:24. Jesus doesn't say, 'you cannot have both God and worldly riches', he says, 'you cannot serve both God and worldly riches'. The problem starts when material possessions go from being useful and enjoyable to being something we treasure more than God – as they had become for the rich young ruler.

Look at Matthew 19:21–22. The young man could not become a follower of Jesus. His heart was being controlled by money leaving no room for Jesus to be Lord.

WHAT'S IT WORTH?

Make a list of all the things you own. Now write a priority number next to each thing on your list to represent how much you value each object – starting at 1 for most important.

Imagine that the top 10 items on your list have been stolen. Write down the emotions you might feel. Would you feel less of a person? Would you feel a part of you had gone with the objects?

Spend some time offering the things on your list to God to use for his cause.

> ### SOLUTION?
>
> Jesus did offer a solution. He said, ' Your heart will be where your treasure is' (Luke 12:34). In other words, although you can' t directly control your heart' s reactions to things or how much you value them, you can strongly influence it by treasuring things God wants you to – and your heart will follow.

THOUGHTS AND THINGS GOD SAID

8. THE GREATEST COMMANDMENT

> **✝ PASSAGE: MATTHEW 22**
> SECTION TO BE READ: MATTHEW 22:34–40

22 A Story About a Wedding Feast

¹ Jesus again used stories to teach the people. He said, ² 'The kingdom of heaven is like a king who prepared a wedding feast for his son. ³ The king invited some people to the feast. When the feast was ready, the king sent his servants to tell the people, but they refused to come.

⁴ 'Then the king sent other servants, saying, "Tell those who have been invited that my feast is ready. I have killed my best bulls and calves for the dinner, and everything is ready. Come to the wedding feast."

⁵ 'But the people refused to listen to the servants and left to do other things. One went to work in his field, and another went to his business. ⁶ Some of the other people grabbed the servants, beat them and killed them. ⁷ The king was furious and sent his army to kill the murderers and burn their city.

⁸ 'After that, the king said to his servants, "The wedding feast is ready. I invited those people, but they were not worthy to come. ⁹ So go to the street corners and invite everyone you find to come to my feast." ¹⁰ So the servants went into the streets and gathered all the people they could find, both good and bad. And the wedding hall was filled with guests.

¹¹ 'When the king came in to see the guests, he saw a man who was not dressed for a wedding. ¹² The king said, "Friend, how were you allowed to come in here? You are not dressed for a wedding." But the man said nothing. ¹³ So the king told some servants, "Tie this man's hands and feet. Throw him out into the darkness, where people will cry and grind their teeth with pain."

¹⁴ 'Yes, many people are invited, but only a few are chosen.'

Is It Right to Pay Taxes or Not?

¹⁵ Then the Pharisees left that place and made plans to trap Jesus into saying something wrong. ¹⁶ They sent some of their own followers and some people from the group called Herodians. They said, 'Teacher, we know that you are an honest man and that you teach the truth about God's way. You are not afraid of what other people think about you, because you pay no attention to who they are. ¹⁷ So tell us what you think. Is it right to pay taxes to Caesar or not?'

¹⁸ But knowing that these leaders were trying to trick him, Jesus said, 'You hypocrites! Why are you trying to trap me? ¹⁹ Show me a coin used for paying the tax.' So the men showed him a coin. ²⁰ Then Jesus asked, 'Whose image and name are on the coin?'

²¹ The men answered, 'Caesar's.'
Then Jesus said to them, 'Give to Caesar the things that are Caesar's, and give to God the things that are God's.'

²² When the men heard what Jesus said, they were amazed and left him and went away.

Some Sadducees Try to Trick Jesus

²³ That same day some Sadducees came to Jesus and asked him a question. (Sadducees believed that people would not rise from the dead.) ²⁴ They said, 'Teacher, Moses said if a married man dies without having children, his brother must marry the widow and have children for him. ²⁵ Once there were seven brothers among us. The first one married and died. Since he had no children, his brother married the widow. ²⁶ Then the second brother also died. The same thing happened to the third brother and all the other brothers. ²⁷ Finally, the woman died. ²⁸ Since all seven men had married her, when people rise from the dead, whose wife will she be?'

²⁹ Jesus answered, 'You don't understand, because you don't know what the Scriptures say, and you don't know about the power of God. ³⁰ When people rise from the dead, they will not marry, nor will they be given to someone to marry. They will be like the angels in heaven. ³¹ Surely you have read what God said to you about rising from the dead. ³² God said, "I am the God of Abraham, the God of Isaac and the God of Jacob." God is the God of the living, not the dead.'

³³ When the people heard this, they were amazed at Jesus' teaching.

The Most Important Command

³⁴ When the Pharisees learned that the Sadducees could not argue with Jesus' answers to them, the Pharisees met together. ³⁵ One Pharisee, who was an expert on the law of Moses, asked Jesus this question to test him: ³⁶ 'Teacher, which command in the law is the most important?'

³⁷ Jesus answered, ' "Love the Lord your God with all your heart, all your soul and all your mind." ³⁸ This is the first and most important command. ³⁹ And the second command is like the first: "Love your neighbour as you love yourself." ⁴⁰ All the law and the writings of the prophets depend on these two commands.'

Jesus Questions the Pharisees

⁴¹ While the Pharisees were together, Jesus asked them, ⁴² 'What do you think about the Christ? Whose son is he?'
They answered, 'The Christ is the Son of David.'

⁴³ Then Jesus said to them, 'Then why did David call him "Lord"? David, speaking by the power of the Holy Spirit, said,

⁴⁴ "The Lord said to my Lord:
Sit by me at my right side,
until I put your enemies under your control."   *Psalm 110:1*

⁴⁵ David calls the Christ "Lord", so how can the Christ be his son?'

⁴⁶ None of the Pharisees could answer Jesus' question, and after that day no one was brave enough to ask him any more questions.

Do you ever worry about what people might say or do when they find out you're a Christian? Do you ever worry that you might not fulfil the greatest commandment in those situations? That's a question young Christians' around the world wrestle with. But the answer varies hugely depending on where you live . . .

ROY'S STORY

In January 1999 a crowd of Christian children and teenagers gathered on the Island of Ambon, Indonesia for a Bible camp. At the end of the week several of the leaders went into the village to rent extra transport for the young people. However, they were attacked by a Muslim mob, stabbed to death and burned. The mob moved towards the site of the Bible camp forcing the children and teenagers to stand before them. Roy Pontoh was 15 years old. He was dragged from his hiding place and told to renounce Jesus or be killed.

Frightened and trembling, Roy nevertheless responded, 'I am a soldier of Christ'.

One of the Muslim attackers swung a sword at his stomach hitting the Bible he held. He swung again and this time sliced open Roy's stomach. Roy's last word was 'Jesus'. His body was dragged out and thrown into a ditch.

Extracted and adapted from Jesus Freaks by DC Talk, published by Voice Of The Martyrs. www.persecution.com

Think: Why do you think Roy didn't give in to their pressure? What do you think motivated him to put his love and loyalty to Christ above his love for his own life?

A TALL ORDER?

Jesus had 613 commands to choose from when picking the greatest command. But he chose this one as the foundation on which all other teaching relies. But what did Jesus mean when he said that his followers have to love him with their heart, soul and mind?

THE HEART

Today the 'heart' means our inner part which feels things. In the Bible it has a much wider meaning. It is the part of us which experiences love and hate, joy and sorrow, peace and bitterness, courage and fear. And it doesn't just feel them, it's the place where we think about these emotions and process them.

THE SOUL

The word 'soul' is first used to describe what happened when God breathed life into Adam – he became a living 'soul' (Genesis 2:7). It's the centre of our personalities, our inner life. And, because it's breathed into by God, it's the part which reflects characteristics of God like love and creativity.

THE MIND

Our minds carry out the intellectual activity, the logical processes and the decisions we make after weighing up the 'fors' and 'againsts'.

Together we are made up of the heart, soul and mind. These control how we use our bodies, energy, creativity and desires – which is why Jesus mentions them here. He's saying that true disciples need to give God all of who they are. God wants total love which dominates our emotions (heart), inner core (soul) and thoughts (mind).

Roy's true story brings this to life. It shows what the greatest commandment looks like when it's lived out in a disciple. It reveals what it means to love God with the soul, mind and strength.

NOT WHERE, BUT WHO

In the Western world it's unlikely that you'll be held at gunpoint for your faith – though it has happened. However, our reactions when we are confronted at school, college or with friends about our faith, give us some idea of how we might react if we were in Roy's shoes.

Britain, America, Burma or Indonesia – it's not *where* we are, but *who* we are.

LISTEN TO THE TRACK > > > > >

If you can, dim the lights and light a candle. The hymn was written more than a thousand years ago but it gets to the heart of what Jesus said about the greatest commandment. Listen to it once letting the words impact you. Then invite God to come and meet with you. Read Matthew 22:37 and talk to God about it. Tell him which areas of your life you most struggle to love him in. Then play the track a second time. As you do ask God to meet with you and give you more love for him.

THOUGHTS AND THINGS GOD SAID

_____

_____

_____

_____

_____

_____

_____

_____

_____

_____

9. JESUS' RETURN

TRACK 9: 'THERE IS A DAY' BY PHATFISH

✝ PASSAGE: MATTHEW 24 & 25
SECTION TO BE READ: MATTHEW 24:36–25:46

24 The Temple will Be Destroyed

[1] As Jesus left the Temple and was walking away, his followers came up to show him the Temple's buildings. [2] Jesus asked, 'Do you see all these buildings? I tell you the truth, not one stone will be left on another. Every stone will be thrown down to the ground.'

[3] Later, as Jesus was sitting on the Mount of Olives, his followers came to be alone with him. They said, 'Tell us, when will these things happen? And what will be the sign that it is time for you to come again and for this age to end?'

[4] Jesus answered, 'Be careful that no one fools you. [5] Many will come in my name, saying, "I am the Christ," and they will fool many people. [6] You will hear about wars and stories of wars that are coming, but don't be afraid. These things must happen before the end comes. [7] Nations will fight against other nations; kingdoms will fight against other kingdoms. There will be times when there is no food for people to eat, and there will be earthquakes in different places. [8] These things are like the first pains when something new is about to be born.

[9] 'Then people will arrest you, hand you over to be hurt, and kill you. They will hate you because you believe in me. [10] At that time, many will lose their faith, and they will turn against each other and hate each other. [11] Many false prophets will come and cause many people to believe lies. [12] There will be more and more evil in the world, so most people will stop showing their love for each other. [13] But those people who keep their faith until the end will be saved. [14] The Good News about God's kingdom will be preached in all the world, to every nation. Then the end will come.

[15] 'Daniel the prophet spoke about "the destroying terror". You will see this standing in the holy place.' (You who read this should understand what it means.) [16] 'At that time, the people in Judea should run away to the mountains. [17] If people are on the roofs of their houses, they must not go down to get anything out of their houses. [18] If people are in the fields, they must not go back to get their coats. [19] At that time, how terrible it will be for women who are pregnant or have nursing babies! [20] Pray that it will not be winter or a Sabbath day when these things happen and you have to run away, [21] because at that time there will be much trouble. There will be more trouble than there has ever been since the beginning of the world until now, and nothing as bad will ever happen again. [22] God has decided to make that terrible time short. Otherwise, no one would go on living. But God will make that time short to help the people he has chosen. [23] At that time, someone might say to you, "Look, there is the Christ!" Or another person might say, "There he is!" But don't believe them. [24] False Christs and false prophets will come and perform great wonders and miracles. They will try to fool even the people God has chosen, if that were possible. [25] Now I have warned you about this before it happens.

²⁶ 'If people tell you, "The Christ is in the desert", don't go there. If they say, "The Christ is in the inner room," don't believe it. ²⁷ When the Son of Man comes, he will be seen by everyone, like lightning flashing from the east to the west. ²⁸ Wherever the dead body is, there the vultures will gather.

²⁹ 'Soon after the trouble of those days,
"the sun will grow dark,
and the moon will not give its light.
The stars will fall from the sky.
And the powers of the heavens will be shaken."   *Isaiah 13:10; 34:4*

³⁰ 'At that time, the sign of the Son of Man will appear in the sky. Then all the peoples of the world will cry. They will see the Son of Man coming on clouds in the sky with great power and glory. ³¹ He will use a loud trumpet to send his angels all around the earth, and they will gather his chosen people from every part of the world.

³² 'Learn a lesson from the fig tree: when its branches become green and soft and new leaves appear, you know summer is near. ³³ In the same way, when you see all these things happening, you will know that the time is near, ready to come. ³⁴ I tell you the truth, all these things will happen while the people of this time are still living. ³⁵ Earth and sky will be destroyed, but the words I have said will never be destroyed.

When will Jesus Come Again?

³⁶ 'No one knows when that day or time will be, not the angels in heaven, not even the Son. Only the Father knows. ³⁷ When the Son of Man comes, it will be like what happened during Noah's time. ³⁸ In those days before the flood, people were eating and drinking, marrying and giving their children to be married, until the day Noah entered the ark. ³⁹ They knew nothing about what was happening until the flood came and destroyed them. It will be the same when the Son of Man comes. ⁴⁰ Two men will be in the field. One will be taken, and the other will be left. ⁴¹ Two women will be grinding grain with a mill. One will be taken, and the other will be left.

⁴² 'So always be ready, because you don't know the day your Lord will come. ⁴³ Remember this: if the owner of the house knew what time of night a thief was coming, the owner would watch and not let the thief break in. ⁴⁴ So you also must be ready, because the Son of Man will come at a time you don't expect him.

⁴⁵ 'Who is the wise and loyal servant that the master trusts to give the other servants their food at the right time? ⁴⁶ When the master comes and finds the servant doing his work, the servant will be blessed. ⁴⁷ I tell you the truth, the master will choose that servant to take care of everything he owns. ⁴⁸ But suppose that servant is evil, and thinks to himself, "My master will not come back soon," ⁴⁹ and he begins to beat the other servants and eat and get drunk with others like him? ⁵⁰ The master will come when that servant is not ready and is not expecting him. ⁵¹ Then the master will cut him in pieces and send him away to be with the hypocrites, where people will cry and grind their teeth with pain.

25 A Story About Ten Bridesmaids

¹ 'At that time the kingdom of heaven will be like ten bridesmaids who took their lamps and went to wait for the bridegroom. ² Five of them were foolish and five were wise. ³ The five foolish bridesmaids took their lamps, but they did not take spare oil for the lamps to burn. ⁴ The wise bridesmaids took their lamps and more oil in jars.

⁵ Because the bridegroom was late, they became sleepy and went to sleep.

⁶ 'At midnight someone cried out, "The bridegroom is coming! Come and meet him!" ⁷ Then all the bridesmaids woke up and got their lamps ready. ⁸ But the foolish ones said to the wise, "Give us some of your oil, because our lamps are going out." ⁹ The wise bridesmaids answered, "No, the oil we have might not be enough for all of us. Go to the people who sell oil and buy some for yourselves."

¹⁰ 'So while the five foolish bridesmaids went to buy oil, the bridegroom came. The bridesmaids who were ready went in with the bridegroom to the wedding feast. Then the door was closed and locked.

¹¹ 'Later the others came back and said, "Sir, sir, open the door to let us in." ¹² But the bridegroom answered, "I tell you the truth, I don't want to know you."

¹³ 'So always be ready, because you don't know the day or the hour the Son of Man will come.

A Story About Three Servants

¹⁴ 'The kingdom of heaven is like a man who was going to another place for a visit. Before he left, he called for his servants and told them to take care of his things while he was gone. ¹⁵ He gave one servant five bags of gold, another servant two bags of gold and a third servant one bag of gold, to each one as much as he could manage. Then he left. ¹⁶ The servant who got five bags went quickly to invest the money and earned five more bags. ¹⁷ In the same way, the servant who had two bags invested them and earned two more. ¹⁸ But the servant who got one bag went out and dug a hole in the ground and hid the master's money.

¹⁹ 'After a long time the master came home and asked the servants what they did with his money. ²⁰ The servant who was given five bags of gold brought five more bags to the master and said, "Master, you trusted me to care for five bags of gold, so I used your five bags to earn five more." ²¹ The master answered, "You did well. You are a good and loyal servant. Because you were loyal with small things, I will let you care for much greater things. Come and share my joy with me."

²² 'Then the servant who had been given two bags of gold came to the master and said, "Master, you gave me two bags of gold to care for, so I used your two bags to earn two more." ²³ The master answered, "You did well. You are a good and loyal servant. Because you were loyal with small things, I will let you care for much greater things. Come and share my joy with me."

²⁴ 'Then the servant who had been given one bag of gold came to the master and said, "Master, I knew that you were a hard man. You harvest things you did not plant. You gather crops where you did not sow any seed. ²⁵ So I was afraid and went and hid your money in the ground. Here is your bag of gold." ²⁶ The master answered, "You are a wicked and lazy servant! You say you knew that I harvest things I did not plant and that I gather crops where I did not sow any seed. ²⁷ So you should have put my gold in the bank. Then, when I came home, I would have received my gold back with interest."

²⁸ 'So the master told his other servants, "Take the bag of gold from that servant and give it to the servant who has ten bags of gold. ²⁹ Those who have much will get more, and they will have much more than they need. But those who do not have much will have everything taken away from them." ³⁰ Then the master said, "Throw that useless servant outside, into the darkness where people will cry and grind their teeth with pain."

The King will Judge All People

[31] 'The Son of Man will come again in his great glory, with all his angels. He will be King and sit on his great throne. [32] All the nations of the world will be gathered before him, and he will separate them into two groups as a shepherd separates the sheep from the goats. [33] The Son of Man will put the sheep on his right and the goats on his left.

[34] 'Then the King will say to the people on his right, "Come, my Father has given you his blessing. Receive the kingdom God has prepared for you since the world was made. [35] I was hungry, and you gave me food. I was thirsty, and you gave me something to drink. I was alone and away from home, and you invited me into your house. [36] I was without clothes, and you gave me something to wear. I was sick, and you cared for me. I was in prison, and you visited me."

[37] 'Then the good people will answer, "Lord, when did we see you hungry and give you food, or thirsty and give you something to drink? [38] When did we see you alone and away from home and invite you into our house? When did we see you without clothes and give you something to wear? [39] When did we see you sick or in prison and care for you?"

[40] 'Then the King will answer, "I tell you the truth, anything you did for even the least of my people here, you also did for me."

[41] 'Then the King will say to those on his left, "Go away from me. You will be punished. Go into the fire that burns forever that was prepared for the devil and his angels. [42] I was hungry, and you gave me nothing to eat. I was thirsty, and you gave me nothing to drink. [43] I was alone and away from home, and you did not invite me into your house. I was without clothes, and you gave me nothing to wear. I was sick and in prison, and you did not care for me."

[44] 'Then those people will answer, "Lord, when did we see you hungry or thirsty or alone and away from home or without clothes or sick or in prison? When did we see these things and not help you?"

[45] 'Then the King will answer, "I tell you the truth, anything you refused to do for even the least of my people here, you refused to do for me."

[46] 'These people will go off to be punished for ever, but the good people will go to live for ever.'

Think about how you see the Second Coming of Jesus. What images do you have of how it will happen? Do you think you'll be ready? What would you have to do to be ready?

Read Matthew 24:36–51.

From what you read, do you think the return of Jesus sounds like something to look forward to, or something to fear? Think about the descriptions used:

- Jesus' return will be like 'the flood' that killed all humans except a handful of righteous people (Matthew 24:39).
- Jesus' return will be sudden. Some people will disappear, some will remain. People won't realise until it has happened (Matthew 24:40).

- Jesus' return will be like a thief coming in the night. It will be sudden and unexpected (Matthew 24:43).
- Jesus return will be a painful event for some (Matthew 24:51).

The descriptions above make it sound like something to fear. However, there is another side to it. Jesus was talking to his followers at a time when they were getting a bit hung up on the times and dates of his return. He needed them to see that the important issue was not *when he* came back (Matthew 24:3) but *whether they* would be ready (Matthew 24:46).

The song you are about to listen to describes the return of Jesus from the perspective of someone who is ready for him . . .

LISTEN TO THE TRACK > > > > >

What do you think makes the difference between those who will be full of fear at Jesus' return and those who will see it as 'a day of freedom and liberation' as the song says?

Read Matthew 25:14–30.

This answers that question – it's the people who are ready for Jesus who will have nothing to fear. Note that it's not the people who show their readiness by sitting around waiting, doing nothing, but those who get on with what God wants them to do.

But what did Jesus say he wants us to do? What criteria will he use to decide?

Read Matthew 25:31–46.

This sums up the criteria on which Jesus will decide who will be with him and who will not. Think about the following questions:

- Who do you think 'the least' are? (See verse 40.)
- Why do you think Jesus compares himself to 'the least'? (See verse 40.)
- Have you ever thought about the idea that when you are serving someone society looks down on, you are serving Jesus?
- Why do you think Jesus is so concerned about what people do for 'the least'?

Think for a minute about how you act when no one else is looking? That's the real you! For example, someone might say they love a certain singer so as not to look like the odd one out. But, if they never listen to that singer's music when they are on their own then the real them probably isn't really into that music.

This is what Jesus is getting at through the sheep and goats story. He's saying that our reaction to the 'least' – people society looks down on, like the homeless or those in prison – shows who we really are. No one applauds you when you give a burger to a homeless person, and they can't repay you. Therefore when we help the 'least' it is coming out of who we really are. It's evidence that God has changed our hearts. And we are doing it for God because he may be the only one who sees.

Think: Jesus is talking here about his return, but what is he focusing our attention on? Look at the following verses for a clue: Matthew 24:46; Matthew 25:13; Matthew 25:20–21; Matthew 25:40. (Jesus is saying that when he returns he wants to find people busy serving him.)

Find some card and write out Matthew 25:37–40 on it. Write the heading 'What Jesus Sees' above it. Decorate it to suit your taste and display it somewhere you will see it each day.

LISTEN TO THE TRACK AGAIN > > > > >

Spend some time talking to God about his return and how you want to live your life in the meantime.

THOUGHTS AND THINGS GOD SAID

_____

_____

_____

_____

_____

_____

_____

_____

---

10. THE LOVE OF GOD

TRACK 10: **'THE CROSS'** BY PHATFISH

 PASSAGE: MATTHEW 26 & 27
SECTION TO BE READ: MATTHEW 26:47–27:66

26 The Plan to Kill Jesus

¹ After Jesus finished saying all these things, he told his followers, ² 'You know that the day after tomorrow is the day of the Passover Feast. On that day the Son of Man will be given to his enemies to be crucified.'

³ Then the leading priests and the older Jewish leaders had a meeting at the palace of the high priest, named Caiaphas. ⁴ At the meeting, they planned to set a trap to arrest Jesus and kill him. ⁵ But they said, 'We must not do it during the feast, because the people might cause a riot.'

Perfume for Jesus' Burial

⁶ Jesus was in Bethany at the house of Simon, who had a skin disease. ⁷ While Jesus was there, a woman approached him with an alabaster jar filled with expensive perfume. She poured this perfume on Jesus' head while he was eating.

⁸ His followers were upset when they saw the woman do this. They asked, 'Why waste that perfume? ⁹ It could have been sold for a great deal of money and the money given to the poor.'

¹⁰ Knowing what had happened, Jesus said, 'Why are you troubling this woman? She did an excellent thing for me. ¹¹ You will always have the poor with you, but you will not always have me. ¹² This woman poured perfume on my body to prepare me for burial. ¹³ I tell you the truth, wherever the Good News is preached in all the world, what this woman has done will be told, and people will remember her.'

Judas Becomes an Enemy of Jesus

¹⁴ Then one of the twelve apostles, Judas Iscariot, went to talk to the leading priests. ¹⁵ He said, 'What will you pay me for giving Jesus to you?' And they gave him 30 silver coins. ¹⁶ After that, Judas watched for the best time to turn Jesus in.

Jesus Eats the Passover Meal

¹⁷ On the first day of the Feast of Unleavened Bread, the followers came to Jesus. They said, 'Where do you want us to prepare for you to eat the Passover meal?'

¹⁸ Jesus answered, 'Go into the city to a certain man and tell him, "The Teacher says: the chosen time is near. I will have the Passover with my followers at your house."'

[19] The followers did what Jesus told them to do, and they prepared the Passover meal.

 [20] In the evening Jesus was sitting at the table with his twelve followers. [21] As they were eating, Jesus said, 'I tell you the truth, one of you will turn against me.'

 [22] This made the followers very sad. Each one began to say to Jesus, 'Surely, Lord, I am not the one who will turn against you, am I?'

 [23] Jesus answered, 'The man who has dipped his hand with me into the bowl is the one who will turn against me. [24] The Son of Man will die, just as the Scriptures say. But how terrible it will be for the person who hands the Son of Man over to be killed. It would be better for him if he had never been born.'

 [25] Then Judas, who would give Jesus to his enemies, said to Jesus, 'Teacher, surely I am not the one, am I?'
Jesus answered, 'Yes, it is you.'

The Lord's Supper

 [26] While they were eating, Jesus took some bread and thanked God for it and broke it. Then he gave it to his followers and said, 'Take this bread and eat it; this is my body.'

 [27] Then Jesus took a cup and thanked God for it and gave it to the followers. He said, 'Every one of you drink this. [28]This is my blood which is the new agreement that God makes with his people. This blood is poured out for many to forgive their sins. [29] I tell you this: I will not drink of this fruit of the vine again until that day when I drink it new with you in my Father's kingdom.'

 [30] After singing a hymn, they went out to the Mount of Olives.

Jesus' Followers Will Leave Him

 [31] Jesus told his followers, 'Tonight you will all stumble in your faith on account of me, because it is written in the Scriptures:
"I will kill the shepherd,
and the sheep will scatter."   *Zechariah 13:7*

 [32] But after I rise from the dead, I will go ahead of you into Galilee.'

 [33] Peter said, 'Everyone else may stumble in their faith because of you, but I will not.'

 [34] Jesus said, 'I tell you the truth, tonight before the cockerel crows you will say three times that you don't know me.'

 [35] But Peter said, 'I will never say that I don't know you! I will even die with you!' And all the other followers said the same thing.

Jesus Prays Alone

 [36] Then Jesus went with his followers to a place called Gethsemane. He said to them, 'Sit here while I go over there and pray.' [37] He took Peter and the two sons of Zebedee with him, and he began to be very sad and troubled. [38] He said to them, 'My heart is full of sorrow, to the point of death. Stay here and watch with me.'

 [39] After walking a little farther away from them, Jesus fell to the ground and prayed, 'My Father, if it is possible, do not give me this cup of suffering. But do what you want, not what I want.' [40] Then Jesus went back to his followers and found them asleep. He said to Peter, 'You men could not stay awake with me for one hour? [41] Stay awake and pray for strength against temptation. The spirit wants to do what is right, but the body is weak.'

⁴² Then Jesus went away a second time and prayed, 'My Father, if it is not possible for this painful thing to be taken from me, and if I must do it, I pray that what you want will be done.'

⁴³ Then he went back to his followers, and again he found them asleep, because their eyes were heavy. ⁴⁴ So Jesus left them and went away and prayed a third time, saying the same thing.

⁴⁵ Then Jesus went back to his followers and said, 'Are you still sleeping and resting? The time has come for the Son of Man to be handed over to sinful people. ⁴⁶ Get up, we must go. Look, here comes the man who has turned against me.'

Jesus is Arrested

⁴⁷ While Jesus was still speaking, Judas, one of the twelve apostles, came up. With him were many people carrying swords and clubs who had been sent from the leading priests and the Jewish elders of the people. ⁴⁸Judas had planned to give them a signal, saying, 'The man I kiss is Jesus. Arrest him.' ⁴⁹ At once Judas went to Jesus and said, Greetings, Teacher! and kissed him.

⁵⁰ Jesus answered, 'Friend, do what you came to do.'
Then the people came and grabbed Jesus and arrested him. ⁵¹ When that happened, one of Jesus' followers reached for his sword and pulled it out. He struck the servant of the high priest and cut off his ear.

⁵² Jesus said to the man, 'Put your sword back in its place. All who use swords will be killed with swords. ⁵³ Surely you know I could ask my Father, and he would give me more than twelve armies of angels. ⁵⁴ But it must happen this way to bring about what the Scriptures say.'

⁵⁵ Then Jesus said to the crowd, 'You came to get me with swords and clubs as if I were a criminal. Every day I sat in the Temple teaching, and you did not arrest me there. ⁵⁶ But all these things have happened so that it will come about as the prophets wrote.' Then all of Jesus' followers left him and ran away.

Jesus Before the Leaders

⁵⁷ Those people who arrested Jesus led him to the house of Caiaphas, the high priest, where the teachers of the law and the older Jewish leaders were gathered. ⁵⁸ Peter followed far behind to the courtyard of the high priest's house, and he sat down with the guards to see what would happen to Jesus.

⁵⁹ The leading priests and the whole Jewish council tried to find something false against Jesus so they could kill him. ⁶⁰ Many people came and told lies about him, but the council could find no real reason to kill him. Then two people came and said, ⁶¹'This man said, "I can destroy the Temple of God and build it again in three days."'

⁶² Then the high priest stood up and said to Jesus, 'Aren't you going to answer? Don't you have something to say about their charges against you?' ⁶³ But Jesus said nothing. Again the high priest said to Jesus, 'I command you by the power of the living God: tell us if you are the Christ, the Son of God.'

⁶⁴ Jesus answered, 'Those are your words. But I tell you, in the future you will see the Son of Man sitting at the right hand of God, the Powerful One, and coming on clouds in the sky.'

⁶⁵ When the high priest heard this, he tore his clothes and said, 'This man has said things that are against God! We don't need any more witnesses; you all heard him

say these things against God. 66 What do you think?'
The people answered, 'He should die.'

67 Then the people there spat in Jesus' face and beat him with their fists. Others slapped him. 68 They said, 'Prove to us that you are a prophet, you Christ! Tell us who hit you!'

Peter Says He Doesn't Know Jesus

69 At that time, as Peter was sitting in the courtyard, a servant girl came to him and said, 'You also were with Jesus of Galilee.'

70 But Peter said to all the people there that he was never with Jesus. He said, 'I don't know what you are talking about.'

71 When he left the courtyard and was at the gate, another girl saw him. She said to the people there, 'This man was with Jesus of Nazareth.'

72 Again, Peter said he was never with him, saying, 'I swear I don't know this man Jesus!'

73 A short time later, some people standing there went to Peter and said, 'Surely you are one of those who followed Jesus. The way you talk shows it.'

74 Then Peter began to place a curse on himself and swear, 'I don't know the man.' At once, a cockerel crowed. 75 And Peter remembered what Jesus had told him: 'Before the cockerel crows, you will say three times that you don't know me.' Then Peter went outside and cried bitterly.

27 Jesus is Taken to Pilate

1 Early the next morning, all the leading priests and elders of the people decided that Jesus should die. 2 They tied him, led him away, and turned him over to Pilate, the governor.

Judas Kills Himself

3 Judas, the one who had given Jesus to his enemies, saw that they had decided to kill Jesus. Then he was very sorry for what he had done. So he took the 30 silver coins back to the priests and the leaders, 4 saying, 'I sinned; I handed over to you an innocent man.'
The leaders answered, 'What is that to us? That's your problem, not ours.'

5 So Judas threw the money into the Temple. Then he went off and hanged himself.

6 The leading priests picked up the silver coins in the Temple and said, 'Our law does not allow us to keep this money with the Temple money, because it has paid for a man's death.' 7 So they decided to use the coins to buy Potter's Field as a place to bury strangers who died in Jerusalem. 8 That is why that field is still called the Field of Blood. 9 So what Jeremiah the prophet had said came true: 'They took 30 silver coins. That is how little the Israelites thought he was worth. 10 They used those 30 silver coins to buy the potter's field, as the Lord commanded me.'

Pilate Questions Jesus

11 Jesus stood before Pilate the governor, and Pilate asked him, 'Are you the king of the Jews?'
Jesus answered, 'Those are your words.'

12 When the leading priests and the elders accused Jesus, he said nothing.

¹³ So Pilate said to Jesus, 'Don't you hear them accusing you of all these things?' ¹⁴ But Jesus said nothing in answer to Pilate, and Pilate was very surprised at this.

Pilate Tries to Free Jesus

¹⁵ Every year at the time of Passover the governor would free one prisoner whom the people chose. ¹⁶ At that time there was a man in prison, named Barabbas, who was known to be very bad. ¹⁷ When the people gathered at Pilate's house, Pilate said, 'Whom do you want me to set free: Barabbas or Jesus who is called the Christ?' ¹⁸ Pilate knew that the people turned Jesus in to him because they were jealous.

¹⁹ While Pilate was sitting there on the judge's seat, his wife sent this message to him: 'Don't have anything to do with that man, because he is innocent. Today I had a dream about him, and it troubled me very much.'

²⁰ But the leading priests and elders convinced the crowd to ask for Barabbas to be freed and for Jesus to be killed.

²¹ Pilate said, 'I have Barabbas and Jesus. Which do you want me to set free for you?' The people answered, 'Barabbas.'

²² Pilate asked, 'So what should I do with Jesus, the one called the Christ?' They all answered, 'Crucify him!'

²³ Pilate asked, 'Why? What wrong has he done?' But they shouted louder, 'Crucify him!'

²⁴ When Pilate saw that he could do nothing about this and that a riot was starting, he took some water and washed his hands in front of the crowd. Then he said, 'I am not guilty of this man's death. You are the ones who are causing it!'

²⁵ All the people answered, 'We and our children will be responsible for his death.'

²⁶ Then he set Barabbas free. But Jesus was beaten with whips and handed over to the soldiers to be crucified.

²⁷ The governor's soldiers took Jesus into the governor's palace, and they all gathered around him. ²⁸ They took off his clothes and put a red robe on him. ²⁹ Using thorny branches, they made a crown, put it on his head, and put a stick in his right hand. Then the soldiers bowed before Jesus and made fun of him, saying, 'Hail, King of the Jews!' ³⁰ They spat on Jesus. Then they took his stick and began to beat him on the head. ³¹ After they finished, the soldiers took off the robe and put his own clothes on him again. Then they led him away to be crucified.

Jesus is Crucified

³² As the soldiers were going out of the city with Jesus, they forced a man from Cyrene, named Simon, to carry the cross for Jesus. ³³ They all came to the place called Golgotha, which means the Place of the Skull. ³⁴ The soldiers gave Jesus wine mixed with gall to drink. He tasted the wine but refused to drink it. ³⁵ When the soldiers had crucified him, they threw lots to decide who would get his clothes. ³⁶ The soldiers sat there and continued watching him. ³⁷ They put a sign above Jesus' head with a charge against him. It said: THIS IS JESUS, THE KING OF THE JEWS. ³⁸ Two robbers were crucified beside Jesus, one on the right and the other on the left. ³⁹ People walked by and insulted Jesus and shook their heads, ⁴⁰ saying, 'You said you could destroy the Temple and build it again in three days. So save yourself! Come down from that cross if you are really the Son of God!'

[41] The leading priests, the teachers of the law, and the Jewish elders were also making fun of Jesus. [42] They said, 'He saved others, but he can't save himself! He says he is the king of Israel! If he is the king, let him come down now from the cross. Then we will believe in him. [43] He trusts in God, so let God save him now, if God really wants him. He himself said, "I am the Son of God."' [44] And in the same way, the robbers who were being crucified beside Jesus also insulted him.

Jesus Dies

[45] At noon the whole country became dark, and the darkness lasted for three hours. [46] At about three o'clock Jesus cried out in a loud voice, 'Eli, Eli, lama sabachthani?' This means, 'My God, my God, why have you rejected me?'

[47] Some of the people standing there who heard this said, 'He is calling Elijah.'

[48] Quickly one of them ran and got a sponge and filled it with vinegar and tied it to a stick and gave it to Jesus to drink. [49] But the others said, 'Don't bother him. We want to see if Elijah will come to save him.'

[50] But Jesus cried out again in a loud voice and died.

[51] Then the curtain in the Temple was torn into two pieces, from the top to the bottom. Also, the earth shook and rocks broke apart. [52] The graves opened, and many of God's people who had died were raised from the dead. [53] They came out of the graves after Jesus was raised from the dead and went into the holy city, where they appeared to many people.

[54] When the army officer and the soldiers guarding Jesus saw this earthquake and everything else that happened, they were very frightened and said, 'He really was the Son of God!'

[55] Many women who had followed Jesus from Galilee to help him were standing at a distance from the cross, watching. [56] Mary Magdalene, and Mary the mother of James and Joseph, and the mother of James and John were there.

Jesus is Buried

[57] That evening a rich man named Joseph, a follower of Jesus from the town of Arimathea, came to Jerusalem. [58] Joseph went to Pilate and asked to have Jesus' body. So Pilate gave orders for the soldiers to give it to Joseph. [59] Then Joseph took the body and wrapped it in a clean linen cloth. [60] He put Jesus' body in a new tomb that he had cut out of a wall of rock, and he rolled a very large stone to block the entrance of the tomb. Then Joseph went away. [61] Mary Magdalene and the other woman named Mary were sitting near the tomb.

The Tomb of Jesus is Guarded

[62] The next day, the day after Preparation Day, the leading priests and the Pharisees went to Pilate. [63] They said, 'Sir, we remember that while that liar was still alive he said, "After three days I will rise from the dead." [64] So give the order for the tomb to be guarded closely till the third day. Otherwise, his followers might come and steal the body and tell people that he has risen from the dead. That lie would be even worse than the first one.'

[65] Pilate said, 'Take some soldiers and go and guard the tomb the best way you know.' [66] So they all went to the tomb and made it safe from thieves by sealing the stone in the entrance and putting soldiers there to guard it.

What you are about to look at is the very heart and centre of the Christian faith. Before you start, spend a few minutes in silence. Tell Jesus he is welcome in your life. Pray that as you learn about his death he will speak to you powerfully.

LISTEN TO THE TRACK > > > > >

As you listen, close your eyes and visualise what is being sung.

There is a lot of material to read here. If you are able, read the full account. If time is short read the abbreviated account:

Full account: Matthew 26:47–27:66
Abbreviated account: Matthew 27:32–61

Think about these questions:

■ If you were Jesus' mother, Mary, or one of the disciples watching Jesus die, would it seem like a demonstration of God's love?

■ The song you heard says: 'My life had its beginning at your cross'. Do you think anyone watching Jesus' crucifixion saw it as a new start for them?

■ What does this say about how we see things and how God sees things?

YOUR VIEW?

There are two ways of looking at Jesus' death: as a believer or as a doubter. Look at Matthew 26:14–16 and Matthew 26:28. Judas was a doubter. He didn't see the bigger plan in it all. Jesus, however, knew there was a bigger purpose, which could only be fulfilled through his suffering. He believed.

The death of Jesus wasn't a random series of gruesome events. It was part of God's plan to bring us close to him – even though it was costly for him. This sort of love is called 'sacrificial love'.

SACRIFICIAL LOVE

Think about a time when you've been willing to accept a cost in order to show love to someone. Maybe you stayed up late one night looking after a sick family member, or spent time helping a friend with homework when you had other (more exciting) things planned. Why did you do it? What were you saying about the person through your actions?

Now think of a time when someone showed sacrificial love to you. How did it make you feel? What were they saying about you through their actions?

Now think about the death of Jesus. Jesus experienced fear, betrayal and anxiety:

- Jesus was scared and didn't want to go through it (Matthew 26:39).
- Jesus' friends didn't do a good job in supporting him (Matthew 26:40–41).
- Jesus was betrayed at his weakest moment by a disciple (Matthew 26:47).

However, something drove him on. What was it? Take a moment to think about this – in the face of fear and betrayal why didn't Jesus quit?

The answer is because of his love for you. Real love is always sacrificial love.

Think about yourself for a moment. Which description best fits you?

A. I find it easier to receive love than to give it.

B. I find it easier to show love to others than to receive it.

IF YOU ANSWERED A, READ THE FOLLOWING:

Jesus set his followers an example when he died. He showed a pattern for how Christians should love – sacrificially. And he showed that although loving other people is sometimes costly, God blesses us when we do it, and by doing it we prove our love is real.

Read Matthew 26:27–28.

LISTEN TO THE TRACK AGAIN > > > > >

Think about Jesus' example of what it means to love others sacrificially.

IF YOU ANSWERED B, READ THE FOLLOWING:

Jesus' death contains a strong message about how deeply he loves you.

Read Matthew 26:27–28. Jesus gave the cup to everyone symbolising that they all needed to receive the sacrifice he was going to make in order to be forgiven and find true life.

LISTEN TO THE TRACK AGAIN > > > > >

Spend some time thinking: you need to receive Christ's love and sacrifice. Open your life to God. Talk to him about his love for you and ask him to help you receive it.

THOUGHTS AND THINGS GOD SAID

_____

_____

_____

_____

_____

_____

_____

_____

_____

_____

YOUTH GROUP
SESSIONS

1.

GOD WITH US

TRACK 1: **'PARALYZED'** BY SIXPENCE NONE THE RICHER

 PASSAGE: MATTHEW 1 & 2

Start by asking the group for feedback from the devotional material they read during the week. Use these questions to stimulate discussion:

- What does the name 'Jesus' mean?
- Do you relate to the idea of feeling paralysed when faced with trying to shine Christ's light on an evil world? Examples?
- Why, when God had worked through prophets for thousands of years, did he decide to come himself?
- What most challenged you or made you think from the study?
- What was 'the incarnation'?

PLAY THE TRACK > > > > >

Explain that we are faced with these kinds of stories of violence, death and destruction every time we open a paper or watch the news. We are going to look at a typical day's news now . . .

CURRENT AFFAIRS

Show five minutes of the news on TV. You'll need to video this one evening in preparation. Try to make sure that some of the stories being covered deal with issues of violence, war, selfishness, destruction and the like.

After showing this, split into groups of three or four. Give each group five minutes to discuss and note down whether they think the widespread wickedness around the world – highlighted in the news they've just seen – proves Jesus failed in his mission to be the 'saviour', and why.

Get their feedback. Then read the following section from the study they did in the week:

In Matthew's gospel Jesus is not described as a police officer or a social worker. He's described as a shepherd – a leader of people. His mission was not to clean up the earth himself, but to empower his followers – us – so that we wouldn't feel paralysed, but could begin to change the world.

Still in their small groups, give them five minutes to discuss who, then, is responsible for the mess the world is in: Politicians? Christians? The European Union? Us?

Allow time for feedback.

GOD WITH US

Explain that you're going to look at what it means that God is now with us and what difference this makes in our lives. Divide off into three groups. Give one of the following to each and suggest they come up with two endings to each scenario: a 'God with us' ending – how they'd act as a Christian, and a 'God not with us' ending – how they'd act if they didn't know God.

GROUP 1

You are shopping. You buy a new hat and pay with a £10 note. The shop attendant seems new and nervous and mistakes your ten for a twenty. She gives you more change than the whole amount you paid with in the first place. You think quickly and decide to . . .

You go to the swimming pool. You're with a friend. You get out and go into the communal shower area. Two older youths enter and start having a laugh at your friend's expense. You know that your friend has low self-esteem and that it would boost their confidence hugely if you stood up for them. You mind is racing and you decide to . . .

GROUP 2

You are at a friend's house. She isn't your closest friend, but has always been loyal to you. Her boyfriend's also there. Your friend goes out to get a video. You chat to her boyfriend and really connect with him. He asks if you'd like to go out next week – just the two of you. You know you'd enjoy spending time with him, but are aware that your friend wouldn't be so happy if she knew. You think fast and decide to . . .

You are hanging around with some friends. It's Saturday evening – there are five lads and five girls. One of the guys gets out a pack of cards and suggests strip poker. You know he means business and don't feel totally comfortable. But to protest would not make you popular. You decide to . . .

GROUP 3

You go to the cinema with a friend. The film you were intending to see is sold out. Your friend wants to see a film which has raised controversy in the media for its raunchy sex scenes, bloody shoot-outs and strong language. Tickets are selling fast and you must decide. You think quickly and decide to . . .

You go to a friend's party. They invite you to their room with three others and start rolling a spliff. It's usually a pretty closed group. They smoke joints together regularly and you feel honoured to have been invited. The joint is offered to you. You say . . .

Come back together and allow time for each group to read the scenarios and explain their two endings.

CLOSE

Draw the meeting together by emphasising that we need to read the Bible regularly so that we become familiar with the way Jesus dealt with situations to help us in our own lives. Read Matthew 5:9 and encourage them that Jesus means 'God Saves' and that he empowers us with his saving power.

2.

TEMPTATION

TRACK 2 : 'STILL BURNING' BY SIXPENCE NONE THE RICHER

 PASSAGE: MATTHEW 3:13–17 & 4:1–25

Start by asking the group for feedback from the devotional material they read during the week. Use these questions to stimulate discussion:

1. What was Jesus' 'formula' for resisting temptation? (Drawing strength from God.)

2. Does God use the temptations and tests we face? How?

3. How did Jesus respond to the temptations he faced?

GOOD OR BAD?

Use the following game to look at how modern society often makes us see hard times as bad times. At one end of the room put a poster up saying 'Good'. At the opposite end display a poster saying 'Bad'. In the middle write 'Both' on a piece of paper. You will shout out a word from the list below. The young people must think fast and decide whether the thing you called out is a good thing, a bad thing, or whether it can be both. They must run to the appropriate place in the room. After each word, ask one or two people why they made the choice they did.

Word list (add your own)

Exams
Cinema
Temptation
Deforestation
Jogging
TV
Global Warming
Sickness
Fox Hunting

After the game, refer to the following, making the point that not all things we see as bad, really are bad:

■ It was the Holy Spirit who took Jesus to be tempted (4:1).

■ Jesus' temptation served as a training for his ministry which he started straight after being tempted (4:17).

TEMPTATION LOCATION

Ask where Jesus was tempted. They may well say the desert. Explain that Jesus' temptation took place in various locations throughout the 40-day period:

1. In a barren desert: deserts were believed to be inhabited by spirits. Many early church leaders went into the desert to develop spiritual disciplines.

2. On a mountain: mountains were the sites of many religious shrines. They were holy places.

3. In a city: in Jerusalem.

Split them into pairs and give them four minutes to discuss what sort of temptations each environment might have created in Jesus e.g. the city may have sparked thoughts of power and wealth.

Allow time for feedback then explain that temptation repeats itself. We are often tempted in similar places, by similar things again and again. If you think about it you may be able to identify some of these locations, for example, when surfing the net, when in a seat at school/college which makes cheating easy, when at a certain club . . .

PLAY THE TRACK > > > > >

Ask them to spend time identifying in their heads some of these places, and to make a decision to avoid them or ask for God's strength when they are next there.

End this section by reading the following quote from Edmund Hillary – the first person to climb Everest. He said, 'It's not the mountain we conquer, but ourselves.' There is an element of truth here. It's not just where we are, but who we are that determines whether we resist temptation. Give out slips of paper with this quote on.

RESISTING TEMPTATION

Close by explaining that one of the best ways to resist temptation is like having a bath: we fight temptation by soaking ourselves in the word of God. Like taking a bath, this means allowing his word to cover us and clean us. Suggest they think about this the next time they take a bath.

HANDOUT

As they leave, hand out copies of the following multiple-choice quiz for them to do in the week to assess their weak areas:

1. The thing which most determines whether I choose God's way in a situation, is

a. what my friends think

b. what I think God wants

c. what my family have taught me

d. my own gut feeling

2. When faced with something which is tempting, but which I know God doesn't want me to do, I usually

a. persevere through the temptation by being strong and focused

b. pray for it to be taken away

c. try to resist, eventually give in, then apologise to God later

d. give in straight away, then regret it and feel I've blown it

3. I usually see temptation as

a. a test God has allowed to help me grow and be strong

b. something from the Devil which I should run from

c. a chance to recall bits of the Bible and prove I can do what God wants

d. something which I need God's help to overcome

4. When I do manage to be strong against temptation and do the right thing, I usually feel

a. stronger spiritually and closer to God

b. worried that I'll never be able to overcome the temptation next time

c. like a spiritual giant – even a little bit proud

d. like I've made another step along the path of faith

SEXUAL PRESSURE

TRACK 3: **'YOU DON'T HAVE TO'** BY THE TRIBE

 PASSAGE: MATTHEW 5:1–32

Start by asking the group for feedback from the devotional material they read during the week. Use these questions to stimulate discussion:

- Who thought any of the Bible passages you read were radical? Why?
- Is it realistic in today's culture to think Christian young people can really be radically different on issues of sex?
- Where do you struggle most to follow Jesus' teaching about being different and distinct?

DISCUSSION

Ask the group to get into same-sex groups of two (or three if there's an odd number). Give each group a sheet of paper with Matthew 5:27–30 on and the following statements. They should discuss them and then feed back whether or not they agree, and why, to the wider group:

- 'Everyone looks at someone of the opposite sex lustfully at some point. Jesus was laying out an aim and an ideal. He didn't expect people to really fulfil it.'
- 'What Jesus means by cutting off the bit of your body that offends you is to remove our bodies from the situation that causes us to use them in sinful ways.'
- 'Jesus was mainly concerned with lust in this passage. He'd be less concerned about a situation that was motivated by love.'

Spend some time after they've fed back giving the biblical response to these statements.

SONG CLIPS

Prior to the meeting go through your own – and some friends' – CD collections. Find as many songs (at least 10) as you can which relate to sex, sexual intimacy, sexual passion etc. They can be by secular artists. As an alternative, or alongside the songs, record a selection of TV adverts which use sex or provocative images to sell a product.

Get the group into two teams, providing each with a metal saucepan and wooden spoon. Appoint a leader for each group then play a clip from the first song or show a clip from the first advert. As soon as someone thinks they know the artist and track (or product being advertised) they must indicate this to their team leader by putting their hand up. The team leader must bang their wooden spoon on the saucepan. When this happens stop the music/advert and ask them for the artist/band and track title – or name of product being advertised. One point is scored for artist/band or product name, and a second for the track title in the case of the music. Award a prize to the winning team.

When all song clips/adverts have been played invite the group to comment on the messages that each song presents. Spend some time analysing the lyrics and messages together, writing up your conclusions on a flip chart. Produce some youth culture-type magazines and a list of films currently on at the cinema. Do the same with these, brainstorming what message is being presented through them.

PLAY THE TRACK > > > > >

As a group analyse its message. Conclude by making the point that Christ's message about sex in Matthew 5 is only revolutionary because today's culture – music, magazines, TV, films – presents an opposite message which we get used to and start to see as normal.

SUBTLE CHANGE

Drive this point home by taking them outside. Ask if anyone has ever seen a tree, flower or blade of grass grow – literally in front of their eyes. Explain that this is like culture. It's always changing and evolving, but it does so slowly and we often forget it's changing around us. It's only by coming back to God's word to find what he says about things that we realise how much culture has shifted.

ACTION PLAN

Get the group back into the pairs they were in earlier and refer to the 'Sliding into Sin' and 'Action Plan' sections they did as part of their study in the week. Give out copies of both these sections to refresh their memories. In pairs they should talk through the area they picked and how far they have got with their action plan. Allow them at least five minutes for this. Encourage the pairs to be accountable to each other on this.

DISTINCT FLAVOUR

Draw the session together by brainstorming any celebrities, pop stars or public figures who were/are radical in their thinking on sex. They might come up with figures like Britney Spears who has in the past claimed to be keeping sex for marriage – although her raunchy videos give a different message.

The group will probably struggle to come up with many. Explain that the reason there seem to be so few is because to be a public figure in popular culture means being part of the norms of that culture to some extent. Very few people are able to stand up for a belief or ideal that is different to the norm. But Christ calls us to do that.

Pass a salt dispenser round and instruct everyone to pour some salt into their hands. As you read Matthew 5:13–16 they should taste the salt as a reminder of the distinct flavour God calls us to be in our lives.

THE KINGDOM OF GOD

TRACK 4: **'GENERATION RISING'** BY THE TRIBE

 PASSAGE: MATTHEW 13:1–58

Prior to the meeting, ask several of the group to prepare a large banner reading: 'A Vision To Be Held Tight and Made Real'. They can do it in any style using any materials as long as it's large (bed sheet sort of size) and readable. Display the banner in the room where you meet.

Start by inviting people to feed back what they learnt about the Kingdom of God from the devotional they read in the week.

Then draw attention to the wall art, explaining that in their devotional they learnt about what the Kingdom was and now you are going to look at how we make it real. Tell them that the phrase on the wall comes from the track you're about to listen to . . .

Before you start the track divide those present into four groups. Allocate one verse of the song to each group (there are four verses) to specifically listen to and note what the message of that verse is. (Note: the song is about getting active with our faith and bringing in the Kingdom.)

PLAY THE TRACK > > > > >

Allow time for feedback and discussion about the song's lyrics and message.

STUDYING THE KINGDOM

Split them into two groups and give each a set of questions.

Note: The answers are in brackets. Don't give these out – keep them back for afterwards.

Group 1

Read Matthew 13:1–9 and discuss the following:

- What do you think the earth represents in the account of the seed on rocky ground? (v.5) [The person that nourishes them – Jesus. These people were not pushing down their roots into Jesus.]

- What do you think the thorny weeds represent, and what is their effect on our effectiveness in the Kingdom? (v.7) [Wealth and materialism – they distract us and destroy our effectiveness for the Kingdom.]

- What was Jesus saying about the nature of the Kingdom of God through the account of the seed on good ground? (v.8) [That the Kingdom of God is about using what we are given to multiply and create more good things.]

Group 2

Read Matthew 13:31–33 and discuss the following:

- What point about the Kingdom do you think Jesus is making by comparing it to the mustard seed? (v.32) [That it starts as a small vision or grain of faith in our lives, but grows into something that has a big impact.]

- What do you think the planting of the mustard seed in the field represents? (v.31) [It indicates that the Kingdom grows out of a love for Jesus which we have to nurture in our hearts.]

- What point about the Kingdom of God is Jesus trying to make by comparing it to yeast? (v.33) [Yeast is the agent in dough that makes it rise. The Kingdom of God is the agent that brings change to the world.]

When the groups are done, come back together and allow time for each to feed back. Ensure all the points in the answers (above) are brought out. Prior to the meeting, print out the following points about God's Kingdom (which come from the study they have just done) onto sheets of card and cut them down to credit card-sized pieces. Give one to each young person, encouraging them to keep it with them as they try to build the Kingdom in their lives:

> *A Vision to Be Held Tight and Made Real*
> *Push down your roots into Jesus*
> *Use the smallest seed of faith to*
> *make the Kingdom real*
> *Avoid being distracted by possessions*
> *Know God's Kingdom is active –*
> *it's a change-agent*

PRAYER

Close by sitting in a circle and inviting each person, if they feel able, to say one way they want to build God's Kingdom this week – or a situation they want to bring the Kingdom's blessing into. Spend time praying as a group for strength for each person to do this.

5.

FAITH

TRACK 5: **'LIVE FOR YOU'** BY RACHAEL LAMPA

PASSAGE: MATTHEW 16:1–28

UNFINISHED SENTENCES

This game will enable the group to open up about faith. Ask them to sit in a circle. Have each of the following statements written on pieces of card:

'If I had the faith to do anything, it would be . . .'

'The biggest test of faith I ever went through was . . .'

'The biggest leap of faith I ever made was . . .'

Hold up the three cards so that the top one is visible. Throw a soft ball into the circle. Whoever catches it has to complete the statement which is showing. They must then throw the ball to someone else. You should display a different sentence which that person must then complete. Repeat the game until everyone has had a go.

DEFINING FAITH

Ask members of the group to read out the definitions of faith which they wrote in the devotional (they will need to have brought their books for this). If they are happy to, ask them to explain a bit about why they wrote it in this way.

BLIND FAITH?

Try to get hold of the film *Indiana Jones and The Last Crusade* in which there is a memorable scene where Harrison Ford has to take a leap of faith onto an invisible, but real path across a valley. Show the clip, then open up the floor for a debate around the statement 'Faith is blind'. Split the group into two. One must prepare arguments for, and one against, then present them to the other side. Each side can question and try to find holes in the opposition's arguments.

Conclude the debate by making the point that faith is blind in that, from a worldly perspective, it's like stepping out blindly – as in the film clip. But faith isn't really blind, because we know the person who will catch us. To highlight this, refer to the following situations in which people had to act blindly, but knew the God they were acting for:

1. Noah was told to make room for his son and his son's wife in the ark. At the time God told him to do this Noah didn't even have a son!

2. Abraham was told by God that, at the age of 99, he and his wife, Sarah, would have a son. Sarah had been unable to have children up until then and laughed when she heard this.

3. Jesus went to the house of a synagogue leader whose daughter had died. The mourners laughed at Jesus when he said she was only asleep (Matthew 9:24) but the father had faith.

BIBLE STUDY

Split the young people into five groups, giving each group (except group 5) the passage and questions on a sheet of paper. Note the special instructions below for group 5:

Group 1 – Faith reveals a deeper meaning
Read Matthew 16:1–12

1. What message did the signs Jesus was doing give about who he was? (v.3)

2. Why do you think the Pharisees couldn't understand the signs?

3. Jesus identified that doubt and disbelief were the problems which the Pharisees had. He described this as 'yeast' (v.11) because of the way yeast works through all the dough when bread is being made. What effect does disbelief have on faith? Why?

4. How might faith have changed these two situations?

Group 2 – Faith comes from God
Read Matthew 16:13–20

1. How do you think God showed Peter Jesus' real identity? (v.16)

2. Jesus talks about a rock in verse 18. Does he mean Peter (Peter means rock) or do you think he means something deeper?

3. Do you think faith comes totally from God? What can we do to develop faith?

Group 3 – Faith is not instant
Read Matthew 16:21–23

1. Peter had just been heavily praised by Jesus (v.17). Then he messed up. What does this teach about faith?

2. Peter's problem seemed to relate to his focus and perspective – he took his eyes off spiritual things and looked at human concerns (v.23). Do you relate to his struggle?

3. What things do you think God sees as important? What are the things humans often see as important? (v.23) Make two lists and compare them.

Group 4 – Faith enables you to take risks
Read Matthew 16:24–28

1. Do you think the way to find life is really to lose it? (v.25) Has this ever been your experience?

2. In today's culture, what do you think it actually means to 'give up the things you want'? (v.24) What are these things?

3. What does it mean to 'give up your life' for Jesus? (v.25)

Group 5 – Faith is based on a person you trust

Youth Leader: Act as if you have lost the questions for this group. Spend a few minutes looking through your bag. Then take the group with you out to the car or to a box of papers, enlisting their help in looking. Keep up the search until the other groups have finished their studies.

Come back together and invite groups 1 to 4 to go through what they discussed. As they do, write the characteristic of faith they have looked at on a flipchart or OHP. Then explain that you have tricked group 5 – there were never any questions. Apologise and give them chocolate bars as a booby prize. Ask whether any of them doubted your sincerity, or thought you were misleading them? Why?

Explain that the key element of faith is knowing the person we put our faith in. Group 5 were prepared to act on what the youth leader said because they knew him/her and therefore had faith in them. Unlike humans, God will never mislead us and it's as we know him that we know the person we are putting our faith in.

PLAY THE TRACK SEVERAL TIMES > > > > >

Invite the group to listen the first time, and then to reaffirm their commitment to living for God as it plays a second time. They can do this by praying short, simple prayers out loud.

6.

BEING TRANSFORMED

TRACK 6: 'UNFORGETFUL YOU' BY JARS OF CLAY

 PASSAGE: MATTHEW 17:1–23

Start by asking the group for feedback from the devotional material they read during the week. Use these questions to stimulate discussion:

■ What did you learn about how your environment changes you?
■ Do you think change in our lives is God's job, our job or a bit of both – and, if so, what's the split?
■ What's the hardest thing, in your opinion, about beginning to change?
■ Did you get any ideas for how to change the bits in you God wants changed?

Run a warm-up game. Invite members of the group to finish the following sentences. Start with one, trying a different sentence when answers dry up:

■ 'If I could change one thing in the world, it would be . . .'
■ 'The biggest area I've contributed to and made a change in the world is . . .'
■ 'When I face change I react in this way . . .'
■ 'The biggest thing I want God to change in me is . . .'

Then open the floor for feedback from the devotional study the group has done in the week.

When contributions dry up make the point that different environments cause different changes. Use the example that if we stay in the sun it causes our skin to go a darker shade, and if we visit a cold environment it causes our skin to goose-bump.

Split the group into two teams and explain that you will call something out – e.g. 'The Sun'. Each team then has a minute to think of as many things that are changed by the object you call out. For 'Sun' the list might include: skin, plants, pace of life . . .

After a minute, each team reads out its list. Words that both teams think of score zero. Words that are legitimate, but that only one team has, score one point.

List of words (add your own)

Winter
Air temperature
Rain
War
Snow
Lightning

CHANGE

Prepare some play-dough prior to the meeting – enough for a fist-sized lump per person.

> *PLAY-DOUGH RECIPE*
> *Mix together 2 cups of flour, 2 cups of water, 2 tablespoons of oil, 2 teaspoons of cream of tartar, 1 cup of salt and some food colouring of your choice. Cook the mixture in a saucepan on a low heat. It will become gooey. When it comes away from the saucepan it is ready to use.*

Give lumps of play-dough to each person. Explain that for the next ten minutes they should try to remain silent and mould their dough into various objects and shapes. As they do they should ask God to show them something in their lives he wants to change. They should then create a shape out of play-dough to represent this thing they think God has brought to their mind that he wants to help them change.

After ten minutes, call a halt. Invite any who want to, to talk about their object. Then carefully put the sculptures aside for later.

Ask a volunteer to read out Matthew 17:1–13.

PLAY THE TRACK > > > > >

Say that the experience on the mountain would have been unforgettable for the disciples. Seeing it would have changed them. That's the key for us too. When we see God in our lives and experience his power and presence it changes us.

Ask them to look at their play-dough shapes. Explain that as they see more of God, his presence will change the areas of their lives which the sculpture represents. An American Quaker and philosopher named Douglas Steere summed this up when he said, 'To come near to God is to change'. Jacob knew this. He met God and wrestled with him, and the experience changed him – he was left with a limp and had his name changed from Jacob to Israel.

Devote the remainder of the meeting to prayer. Make sure everyone has their play-dough sculpture in front of them. Encourage everyone to invite God to draw near to them. And suggest they spend time waiting quietly and listening to God. When they feel ready they should talk to God about the thing he wants them to change in their lives. As a symbol of his power to do this they should re-shape their play-dough into a cross.

MATERIALISM

TRACK 7: **'TREASURE'** BY IONA

 PASSAGE: MATTHEW 19:13–30

Spend some time getting feedback and reactions to the devotional study. Read the study yourself beforehand and ask some probing questions. It may have stirred up some strong feelings. Use these as discussion starters.

PLAY THE TRACK > > > > >

Draw out a few of the points made:

- It's God who is saying: 'You are precious to me'. He wants to be the thing we treasure.
- He's given us the flowers and birds as reminders that he can provide and make things beautiful without the help of wealthy donors.
- God loves us. If we ask for bread, he won't give us a stone.

TRUE OR FALSE?

Give everyone a red balloon and a green balloon then split the group into two teams. After everyone has inflated and tied their balloons, explain that you are going to read out a statement about the divide between the wealthy and the poor. After reading each statement everyone will have ten seconds to decide if they think it is true of false. You then shout 'answers' and each person must hold up their green balloon if they think its true and their red if they think its false. There must be no conferring between team members.

Count up how many greens and reds there are in each team. The team that wins each round is the one that has the most correct answers, shown by the balloons.

Questions:

- 80 per cent of the world's diseases occur in poor countries, but only 10 per cent of money spent on health care across the world is spent in poor nations. (*True*) [Source: World Bank].

- Sales of fat-free and diet foods – luxury, not essential foods – in the US amount to $9 billion a year. This is the same as Mali's total GDP. (*True*) [Source: *CIA World Factbook* & *Slimming Market Report*.]

- When Jesus said the poor would always be with us, he meant that that was their place in life – some are rich, some are poor. (*False – he probably meant some men's greed would keep them poor.*)

- Between them, the world's 11 richest people have more money than the combined GDP of the 49 least developed nations on earth. (*True*) [Source: World Bank & *Forbes' Richest People.*]

- In rich countries less than 8 per cent of all children are malnourished. In poor countries around 40 per cent are. (*False – it's 5 per cent and 50 per cent*) [Source: UNHDR 2000/01.]

- Over 1 million people lack access to safe water and over 2 million have no sanitation. (*False – water is 1 billion and sanitation is 2.4 billion*) [Source: Tearfund.]

- In Old Testament times God ordered that there be a jubilee year every fiftieth year when all lands which had been given over to pay debts were returned and people who had sold themselves as slaves to pay debts, were freed. (*True*) [Source: Leviticus 25.]

DRAMA

Ask for a volunteer to read out Matthew 19:16–24. In their same two teams, the young people have twenty minutes to plan a modern-day adaptation of the rich young ruler's encounter with Jesus. The young man might be a nightclub owner, a head teacher, an MP, a journalist. They could be a young woman rather than a young man. The only elements of the story which must remain the same are:

- the young ruler's interest in spirituality (v.16).
- the response of Jesus which must include the need for the putting aside wealth and helping the poor (v.21).

Allow time for each group to perform their sketch.

ACTION PLAN

Wrap up by explaining that action is what counts when dealing with these issues. As a group, discuss and brainstorm ideas to help live out the issues of not being controlled by money but using it to help the poor, which Jesus highlights. Using the following questions to kick start, write a group action plan listing things you will do. An example is to get information on Tearfund's 'Children At Risk' programme and begin supporting and learning about it: www.tearfund.org.

1. How do we overcome our natural inclination to depend on our money and possessions rather than God?

2. How do we overcome our natural inclination to forget about certain nations in Africa, Asia and Latin America where some people could be saved from death for as little as £10 of our money?

THE GREATEST COMMANDMENT

TRACK 8: **'BE THOU MY VISION'** BY FERNANDO ORTEGA

 PASSAGE: MATTHEW 22:34–40

Start the session by inviting any feedback from the devotional study the young people did during the week. What impacted them? Were they challenged by Roy's story? Why? When comments dry up, ask different members of the group to complete the following sentence: 'The biggest thing God asks his followers to do is . . .'

Read Matthew 22:34–40

Brainstorm as a group what it means in life today to love God with all your heart, soul and mind. If you have access to a video camera (or a tape recorder), go around the congregation at your church one Sunday prior to this session asking people to complete the following sentence: 'In my daily life, Jesus' command that we must love with our heart, soul, mind and strength means . . .'

Play the responses after the group have brainstormed their own ideas.

STAND BY YOUR FAITH?

Explain that you're going to look at two situations in which you might be called on to stand by your faith and demonstrate your love for God. Split the group into pairs, giving each pair a copy of both scenarios below. Tell them they should discuss each situation and consider how God might want them to react bearing in mind Matthew 22:37:

> You are in town with several friends. You bump into a guy who knows you are a Christian but doesn't have much faith himself. Another lad, Paul, is with him. Your friend introduces you to Paul. During the conversation your friend asks you something about church. Paul leaps in, announcing he's an atheist and that anyone who believes in God, an afterlife or human need for forgiveness deserves to be sent to an asylum. You respond by . . .

> You are on a summer mission trip to South Africa helping carry out renovation work for a local Christian mission. You start playing football with several local Muslim youths in the evenings. One evening one of them invites you back to their home. You and a friend go and meet the young person's family. All's going well until you mention you are on a Christian mission. The father of the family loses his temper accusing Christianity of creating apartheid and saying Christianity is a lie and Christians are deceived, and challenging you to prove your intelligence by renouncing your 'racist' faith. You respond by . . .

Allow time for each pair to feed back.

PLAY THE TRACK > > > > >

Introduce it by saying that it sums up what it means to live out Matthew 22:37. When it's finished, read the following lists of ways the song mentions that we can love God with all we are:

Verse 1:

- God as our vision for life
- God in our thoughts
- God's presence guiding us wherever we go

Verse 2:

- God as our wisdom and truth
- God always close to us, and us to him
- God as our father and us his children
- God living in us

Verse 3:

- Wealth or public praise not needed – God is enough
- God being first in our hearts
- God as our treasure

Verse 4:

- God as our future hope in heaven
- God as our strength through whatever we go through
- God giving us his vision for life

Split the group into four teams, allocating a verse to each. They must pick a key theme from their verse using the above list and then interpret it artistically in some way. Provide four sheets or rolls of wallpaper. Make sure each group discusses which theme they will pick up on and talks as a team about how they will interpret it. Along with sheets/wallpaper, provide spray cans, paint, scissors and marker pens.

PRAYER

Wrap things up by getting each group to pray for each other, focusing their prayers on the theme which they painted around. Have the track playing in the background as they pray.

9.

JESUS' RETURN

 PASSAGE: MATTHEW 24:36–25:46

Start by handing out pens and paper and inviting everyone to think about the following scenario: You are stuck on a desert island where you must spend the rest of your life. You're allowed any three wishes (apart from wishing to leave the island). Write them down.

Allow everyone to feed back their wishes. Then make the point that these wishes reveal something about how we like to use our time (refer to several people's wishes to prove the point). In the passage you're about to read, Jesus is talking about the future and his return. However, he ties it strongly into how we use our time now.

Read Matthew 24:36–25:46 as a group.

Then split into two groups, giving one of the following sets of questions to each:

Group 1
Read Matthew 24:36–44

1. What do you think Jesus is saying his followers must always be ready for? (See verse 42.)

2. Do you find it easy or hard to 'always be ready'?

3. What are some common barriers to 'always being ready' ?

4. Brainstorm some practical things/strategies you might find helpful in 'always being ready'.

Group 2
Read Matthew 25:1–13

1. The lamps of the foolish bridesmaids were not alight when the bridegroom returned. What do you think the lamps represent?

2. Keeping a lamp prepared and ready is like keeping our lives prepared and ready. How can we do that?

3. What were the consequences for those whose lamps weren't alight when Jesus came? (See verses 11–12.) Do you think that is a bit harsh?

4. What point do you think Jesus is making through this story? (See verse 13.)

EXPECTANT GAME

Get the group in a circle and pick two people to stand in the centre. 'Player A' must keep a totally straight face, not blinking or twitching. 'Player B' must also keep a straight face. At a time of their own choosing, 'player A' must break the stillness, and try to cause a reaction in 'player B's' face by suddenly shouting 'Boo', laughing, roaring or doing some other unexpected movement. Explain to 'player B' that this will happen and that they must try not to react in any way when the noise comes. The only rule is that players must keep full eye contact.

Play the game several times, involving different pairs. When a 'player B' succeeds in keeping a straight face, allow other people to have a go at trying to cause a reaction in them. You must ensure that there is at least ten seconds of waiting before 'player A' creates their sudden movement.

When the game is over, ask those who were 'player Bs' how they felt. Were they on tenterhooks, in suspense, expectant? How did they prepare for the reaction they knew was coming? Were they focused solely on the sudden movement they were anticipating?

Make the point that Jesus wants us to use our time well while we wait for him, and that part of this is always being expectant that he will return.

PLAY THE TRACK > > > > >

At around 4 minutes 30 seconds into the song there is a 50-second instrumental section. During this read out Matthew 25:13 several times.

> 'So always be ready, because you don't know the day or the hour the Son of Man will come.'
>
> Matthew 25:13

True/False Quiz

Round up with a quiz. Get the group back into two teams and give each a saucepan and wooden spoon. Read each question below and explain that as soon as either team thinks they know the answer they must bang their saucepan to indicate this.

1. Although the phrase 'the Second Coming' is frequently used today to describe Christ's return, it was never actually used in the New Testament. *(True)*

2. Neither Jesus, the Holy Spirit nor God knows when Jesus will come again. *(False – God knows)*

3. Jesus said that when he would come again was not our problem. Our job was to serve him until he did. *(True)*

4. It's believed Jesus will probably come again around Easter time – to tie in with the month he was killed. *(False)*

5. The night before he was killed, Jesus told his followers he would return. *(True – John 14:3)*

6. Christ's return is referred to over 300 times in the New Testament. *(True)*

7. After Jesus went into heaven two angels appeared to his followers promising he would return in the same way. *(True – Acts 1:11)*

8. Theologians have worked out that Christ is likely to come back in 2049. *(False)*

PLAY THE TRACK AGAIN > > > > >

As the music plays invite people to speak out prayers asking God for his help to be always ready for Christ's return.

10.

THE LOVE OF GOD

TRACK 10: **'THE CROSS'** BY PHATFISH

 PASSAGE: MATTHEW 26:47–27:66

The song by Phatfish is a very powerful one. Make the most of it by spending time getting the venue ready. Make a simple cross before the meeting. Have it displayed centrally with several lamps spotlighting it. Keep the rest of the room fairly dim so that the focus is on the cross.

Invite the group to sit quietly as they arrive. Have the following phrases (taken from the song) written up on paper and displayed around the room:

'My life had its beginning at your cross'

'You were my substitute'

'You were crushed by my sin'

PLAY THE TRACK >>>>>

Have the song set to loop on your CD player, or just start it again when it finishes. Invite the group to speak out prayers of thanks as it plays a second time.

Read Matthew 26:26–30 and Matthew 27:32–50.

Explain that communion/the Lord's Supper was established by Jesus at this time. If appropriate for your young people/church, have communion together as a group. As you do, play the track as background sound. If communion isn't appropriate, use the time to explain what communion is, and its significance.

Follow this by splitting the group into three, giving the following phrases (taken from the song) to each group and inviting them to use these as a stimulus for thanking God for what he has done:

- 'The cross where you've broken Satan's back'
- 'Your punishment has brought me peace'
- 'By the wounds you suffered I'm alive and healed'

Wrap this section up by moving the lamps which are spotlighting the cross. Explain that the cross is now empty. It's a key symbol, but that is all it is. The living power of the cross is in Jesus who was resurrected. Ask where Jesus is now. Allow time for discussion around what it means that Jesus now lives in the hearts of his followers.

You may at this point want to invite any feedback from the devotional the young people did in the week. Use the following to stimulate feedback:

1. What is sacrificial love?

2. Do you find it easier to give, or receive love?

3. The line: 'My life had its beginning at your cross'. Do you think anyone watching Jesus' crucifixion saw it as a new start for them?

SYMBOLIC CROSS

Split the group into two and brainstorm the following questions:

- What does the cross symbolise today? *(Sign of religiosity; worn as jewellery.)*
- What did the cross symbolise in Bible times? *(An instrument of torture and death – the equivalent of the gallows or electric chair. Enemies of the state and criminals were executed on crosses as a way of humiliating, torturing and subjecting them to public disgrace as they died.)*
- What does the cross mean for followers of Jesus? *(Forgiveness, hope, love.)*
- What elements of the cross affect the way disciples live their lives?

Come back together and allow time for feedback and discussion.

COLLAGE CROSS

Have a pile of fairly up-to-date magazines and newspapers, along with some plain paper, biros and marker pens at the ready. If possible, get hold of two planks of wood and nail them into the shape of a cross (ideally about 5ft high). If it's easier, use two lengths of wallpaper to create a cross shape.

Give the group ten minutes to look through the magazines and newspapers and cut out pictures or stories of any situations that need the love of God and the healing and forgiving power of the cross in them. They may also wish to write or draw a picture on the plain sheets of paper to represent any situations closer to home which they want to lay before the cross.

When they have done this, invite them to stick the articles and pictures they've cut out and any things they've drawn onto the cross. Then invite them to take a marker pen and write a short prayer over the different situations which they stuck up, asking Jesus to bring the power of the cross into the situation.

WE LOVE BECAUSE CHRIST LOVED

Wrap up by producing a bundle of pieces of wood, some pens and sticky labels. You'll need enough wood for each member of the group to have two pieces. They can be off-cuts – either new or reclaimed, or small branches. They need to be shaped in a way that when two are hammered together they will create the shape of a cross. Also, have several hammers and a pile of nails in the centre.

Invite everyone to find two pieces and nail them into a cross shape. Hand out a sticky label and pen to each person and get them to write down one thing they have learnt about the cross on the label and stick it on their cross. It might be, 'Love must be sacrificial', 'The cross is about receiving love', or 'The cross brings my forgiveness'.

CREDITS

'Paralyzed' – taken from the album *Divine Discontent* by Sixpence None the Richer (Word Entertainment, 2002). Matt Slocum. © Squint Songs, My So-Called Music (admin. by Squint Songs).

'Still Burning' – taken from the album *Divine Discontent* by Sixpence None the Richer (Word Entertainment, 2002). Words by Matt Slocum, music by Matt Slocum and Sean Kelly. © Squint Songs, My So-Called Music (admin. by Squint Songs) O Kelly Songs (admin. by Bug Music).

'You Don't Have To' – taken from the album *Take Back the Beat* by The Tribe (Alliance Music, 2001). BabyDoll, Delport, Mhondera, Owen, Porter, Wanstall, West. © 2001 Perfect Music UK/Alliance Media (admin. by CopyCare).

'Generation Rising' – taken from the album *Take Back the Beat* by The Tribe (Alliance Music, 2001). Porter and Thomas. © 2001 Perfect Music UK/Alliance Media (admin. by CopyCare).

'Live for You' – taken from the album *Live for You* by Rachael Lampa (Word Entertainment, 2000). Chris Eaton and Chris Rodriguez. © 2000 Dayspring Music, Inc./SGO Music Publishing/Still Working For The Man Music, Inc.

'Unforgetful You' – taken from the album *If I Left the Zoo* by Jars of Clay (Essential, 1999). Dan Haseltine, Matt Odmark, Stephen Mason, Charlie Lowell. © 1999 Bridge Building Music, Inc./Pogostick Music/BMI (admin. by Brentwood Benson Music Publishing, Inc).

'Treasure' – taken from the album *The River Flows* by Iona (Open Sky, 2002). Iona. © 1992 SGO Music Management.

'Be Thou My Vision' – taken from the album *The Breaking of the Dawn* by Fernando Ortega (Word Entertainment, 1998). Eighth-century Irish hymn arranged by Fernando Ortega and John Andrew Schreiner. © 1998 MargeeDays Music (admin. by Dayspring Music, Inc.)/Dayspring Music, Inc/John Andrew Schreiner.

'There is a Day' – taken from the album *Heavenbound* by Phatfish (Word Entertainment, 2001). Nathan Fellingham. © Kingsway's Thankyou Music.

'The Cross' – taken from the album *Heavenbound* by Phatfish (Word Entertainment, 2001). Michael Sandeman. © Kingsway's Thankyou Music.